Diversity,
Globalization,
and the
Ways of Nature

D1319132

Diversity, Globalization, and the Ways of Nature

Danilo J. Anton

INTERNATIONAL DEVELOPMENT RESEARCH CENTRE
Ottawa • Cairo • Dakar • Johannesburg • Montevideo • Nairobi
New Delhi • Singapore

Published by the International Development Research Centre
PO Box 8500, Ottawa, ON, Canada K1G 3H9

Anton, D.J.

Diversity, globalization, and the ways of nature. Ottawa, ON, IDRC, 1995.
xi + 223 p. : ill.

/Environmental degradation/ , /environmental management/ , /biodiversity/ ,
/ecological balance/ , /internationalization/ — /forests/ , /grasslands/ , /aquatic
environment/ , /water resources/ , /air quality/ , /energy resources / , /Africa/ ,
/Latin America/ , /Caribbean/ , /urban environment/ , /decentralization/ ,
bibliography.

UDC: 574   ISBN: 0-88936-724-8

A microfiche edition is available.

IDRC BOOKS endeavours to produce environmentally friendly publications. All
paper used is recycled as well as recycleable. All inks and coatings are vegetable-
based products.

Contents

....

Foreword

....

Today, when someone speaks about natural diversity, the image most often evoked is that of the tropical rain forest. On the subject of globalization, the first image might be the logo of CNN, the first worldwide television network. In this book — *Diversity, Globalization, and the Ways of Nature* — Danilo J. Anton shares with us a different perspective: that of a geographer. He teaches us that the rain forest is not alone: there is also diversity in the savannas, in the oceans, and in the myriad of cultures that have developed as humans interact with their ecosystems. He shows us that globalization is a process much more dangerous than has been suggested by some contemporary prophets, who promise a new world transformed into a happy and well-connected "global village."

Anton's vision is, indeed, global. It encompasses all the planet, a large part of which the author knows personally, not as a tourist or neutral onlooker but as an actual agent of transformation and sustainable development. And what Anton sees in all the corners of this diverse world is a systematic aggression against diversity, both natural and cultural — a destructive and impoverishing trend toward uniformity, which hides its threatening face behind the name "globalization."

This book is not a conservative discourse against progress; nor is it a romantic defense of an idyllic past. With scientific accuracy, Anton studies the extraordinary conditions that made possible life on Earth, which were also largely the result of life itself. Our living planet produces the oxygen that makes life possible, while preventing the accumulation of excessive oxygen, which, left unchecked, could result in a planetary inferno. In much the same way, diversity is a consequence of adaptation to the environment, and, at the same time, promotes new adaptations through continuous cross-fertilization. Without their "wild" cousins, the domesticated and genetically impoverished plants that we eat would be unable to resist new plagues or environmental change. In a culturally uniform, "happy" world, the birth of new ideas would be impossible. Diversity is life; uniformity, therefore, is synonymous with death.

Globalization began about 500 years ago with the conquest of America by the empires of Europe. Whereas other "global" empires — such as the Chinese, Incas, and Romans — predated this period, it was the European empires that first opened global markets, reoriented local production, and altered cultures and natural environments to a degree and depth never dreamt of by Alexander the Great or Genghis Khan.

Danilo Anton explores this history from new vantage points:

- The thirst for gold of the conquistadors has been transformed into the thirst for water in the megalopolises of the developing world.

- Irrigation and hydroelectric plants in Africa, the "cradle of humanity," promote desertification instead of helping development.

- In South America, Australian trees may feed the hunger of computers and fax machines for paper, but they also modify the water cycle and provide nesting places for deadly plagues.

With rigour, erudition, and an entertaining style, Anton demonstrates how globalization is the main contemporary force producing uniformity and, therefore, ruin. However, he also illustrates how the same informatics revolution that promotes globalization provides new methods for public participation, the rescue of traditional knowledge, and the defense of the natural environment. This book and its author, therefore, are hopeful. After demonstrating that change is essential, Anton conveys, in the final chapter, his confidence that it is also possible. Strategies for the future should be based on three pillars: decentralized decision-making, community participation in designing activities affecting the environment, and the recognition that global problems affect us all.

Finally, it remains clear that the principal responsibility for these problems falls to the richer countries, which have been the main contributors in their creation. In other words, the thirst for justice must also be quenched.

Roberto Bissio
• Executive Director, Third World Institute
• Editor, *Third World Guide*

December 1994

1

Introduction
....

Globalization and the ways of nature

Trends toward globalization are changing the world. Information systems are allowing the inexpensive generation, processing, and rapid communication of facts, news, data, and ideas throughout the world almost instantaneously. The financial sector is becoming a worldwide web, in which economic and financial decisions are made at a moment's notice and have almost immediate impact. Transportation systems have become fast, standardized, and less expensive. Trade relations have become all encompassing and flexible as capital and products cross national borders with increasing ease.

The increasingly integrated "new order" is having a strong impact on the distribution of economic roles in the world. Sites of investment and production are moved from place to place to maximize cost-effectiveness and convenience. Mexico's *maquiladoras* are assembling American computers, Chinese factories are manufacturing Japanese toys, and Egyptian workers are producing French garments.

These changes are having important effects on societies and environments. One is the growing trend toward uniformity and standardization. Diversity is being severely threatened.

From an environmental point of view, human activities are becoming less and less sustainable. Monoculture based on exotic species and the use of chemical fertilizers and pesticides is affecting ecosystems, soils, and water-distribution patterns. Mining is causing land degradation. Widespread burning of fossil fuels is slowly modifying the Earth's atmosphere.

The planet is changing, and it is losing the flexibility provided by its diversity. Humankind is also squandering its richness, its cultures, its proven traditional production systems — the wealth of experience accumulated throughout history. To address these issues, we must optimize our ability to build on relevant knowledge, keeping in mind that the present is not only the boundary between the past and the future, but also the time to choose successful strategies for survival.

The new globalization processes

Globalization processes have existed since the dawn of the "modern" era. They began as a result of the growth of the first colonial empires, such as those of England, Spain, and France; the worldwide establishment of commercial networks (controlled, more or less, by political or military powers); the opening of new markets in peripheral areas; and the extraction of raw materials for various purposes, including industrialization.

The development of steamboats, trains, and the telegraph during the 19th century facilitated the globalization trend. Later, the invention and spread of new telecommunications systems — such as the telephone, the radio, and, more recently, television — permitted a quantum leap toward a more unified planet. These developments, however, seem to have represented only the beginning of a much bigger process that is only now becoming defined.

During the last few years, as a result of technological advances (computers, facsimile transmission, satellite communications) and the reorganization of the international framework of economies, societies,

Before the electrical telegraph was invented, France had developed its own optical telegraph, which "transmitted" through a series of towers, each 5 to 10 kilometres apart, such as the one shown here in Col de Saverne, France.

and states, profound changes with widespread socioeconomic effects have taken place. Macroeconomic trends are affecting local and regional environments and societies, while processes and activities at a local level are having global environmental and social impacts. New ideas permeate the global culture, changing patterns at all levels. Traditional cultures are being attacked by forces of uniformity, but they are also fighting back using the most modern technological means.

In light of these developments, new questions need to be formulated:

- How do we make sense of the myriad, apparently contradictory signals?

- What is, and will be, the effect of these changes on the environment and the ways of life of people in local communities?

- What is the destiny of nation-states?

- Are we witnessing the birth of a new global culture, or perhaps
  more accurately, a global intelligence?

- What is the destiny of the planet's diversity — both natural and
  social?

- Will the forces of uniformity create the nightmarishly homogeneous, standardized world that has been a frequent scenario in
  science-fiction novels?

Obviously, there are no easy answers to these questions. The purpose of this book is to address some aspects of these issues, particularly
in relation to their effect on environmental management of the planet.
The basic hypothesis is that the new era will have enormous effects on
the human and natural environment, and not necessarily all negative.

2

Global Trends and Their Effects
on the Environment

The information revolution

The end of the 20th century is characterized by a profound technological revolution that has profound effects on the environment and the socioeconomic state of the world. It has been referred to as the "information age," the "third wave" (Toffler 1981), and the "post-industrial society" (Bell 1973). I believe the term "information revolution" is more appropriate.

The two major phenomena promoting this revolution are the development and increasing use of computers, which make possible the storage and processing of large volumes of information, and new telecommunications technologies, which permit the transmission of this information over long distances almost instantaneously. This technology is being integrated to produce powerful tools and systems, increasing by several orders of magnitude humankind's capacity for collective memory and providing a worldwide arena for social interaction. In addition, these systems have become inexpensive, require a small amount of

5

energy and human effort to use, and are becoming more accessible to more and more people all over the world.

The information–telecommunications revolution is generating a "global intelligence" — a computerized neural network with increasing numbers of information producers and users. The producers are not only the public and private institutionalized information packaging and delivery systems, but also scores of smaller groups and individuals with computer terminals and the will to be connected to networks. Consequently, billions of bytes of information are being exchanged every minute among information producers, relay stations, and users and receivers of various kinds.

Along with these advances, and in large measure as a result of them, accessory facilities for production and reproduction of information and ideas, such as photocopiers, home printers, and faxes, have become widely available. Using these resources, many more social groups are now able, even at the local level, to express themselves in new and complex ways — electronic bulletin boards, community newspapers, and local cable television channels. At the national level, too, media are developing locally customized views.

General effects of the information revolution

The global networks provide wider public access to more sources of information than ever before, not only from central information streams, but also from myriad local sources. The possibilities for interaction are multiplying accordingly. Many social contacts are becoming independent of distance, giving rise to a new spectrum of relations that were not previously possible. Internet, the worldwide computer network, currently links more than 20 million users and is growing at a rate of 20% per month! It was built in an extemely democratic fashion, following the basic principles of decentralization, unlimited and total access, and freedom of information (see Elmer-Dewitt 1994). Although it is not yet clear if the Internet will remain a central element of the information age over the long term, it definitely appears that it will continue to play a key role in the development of new social tools of communication for some time to come.

One overall effect of the information revolution appears to be a general democratization of information flow, both at the producer and at the receiver ends, with loss of power by the monopolistic information holders. The increasing availability of knowledge, technical and non-technical, about how to get things done is particularly important. We assume (and hope) that information networks will remain free of control or censorship by any existing or newly created "information power" as has often been the case in the past.[1] Keeping them open is going to be a ongoing global challenge.

The information revolution will probably also result in increasing diversification of expressed points of view and approaches. This diversification effect is critical. In fact, it may be the most effective antidote to the forces of uniformity that are coming into play in the globalized world.

The complex processes of globalization have promoted the development of a mainstream standardized culture that includes not only widespread homogenization of production and consumption systems and patterns, but also greater cultural uniformity, including expression codes, attitudes, and beliefs. The new trend toward diversification and differentiation is building on the flow of information that allows freer expression of alternative perspectives, including those of social minorities and disadvantaged groups who are finding relevant and accessible channels for expressing their opinions and disseminating information.

The creation of new methods for public participation is producing an immense potential for the generation and use of knowledge and innovation at the grass-roots level. Many traditions that had been eliminated, forgotten, or discredited by mainstream culture may now be revived. Traditional knowledge can be rescued, revived, adapted, and sustained.

---

[1] Control of information for political purposes was common during the Cold War and, in large measure, still is today. Major world powers have strongly influenced the flow of news through press agencies that, often subtly, censor "inconvenient" information. Information is also controlled by the use of "authorized" television networks, which are regularly used as political tools both by governments and by wealthy elites.

The more marginalized aspects of complex cultures, often inten-
tionally or by omission wiped out by the forces of standardization, may
also stand a chance of survival if enough of their representatives are
determined to use these newly developing mechanisms. In all likelihood, meso- and microcultures (as well as subcultures) will survive at a
different level than the mainstream culture. The future coexistence of
several cultures, on different planes or levels, will likely become more
common and important. Smaller, usually weaker cultures should be able
to transcend their limited spheres, however, to claim more extended
"virtual" territories. People will be able to belong to a specific culture
without abandoning their rights as part of the wider standard culture.

The potential of this development is enormous. People will be able
to become more homogeneous on one level, but increasingly heteroge-
neous on another. Meso- and microcultures and nations will no longer
disappear under the shadow of a mainstream culture. The industrial
nation-state that has arisen through the smothering of less powerful
national or local groups will lose its main source of power. Unavoidably,
this will lead to fragmentation of power and perhaps instability; but it
will surely lead to more and different forms of democratization as well.

Effects on environmental management

Processes that degrade the environment have often developed as a
result of central decisions based on the views of powerful groups about
how to control or use natural (and human) resources and territory.
Typically, in the centralized industrial states of the world, local groups
are among the least powerful; their environments and cultures are often
undermined or destroyed without their being able to do anything about
it. The reigning ideology tends to equate almost any transformation of
nature with progress and progress with modernization, and assumes that
both are desirable. In consequence, local communities must often
choose between their immediate convenience, on the one hand, and
their long-term welfare, on the other. To make matters worse, they
have little accurate information about the potential long-term effects of
proposed natural and sociocultural transformations.

Even where communities do not agree with proposed measures, they often have few effective channels through which to communicate their views. The right of communities to define their own destinies has not been properly acknowledged in practice, even when present in policy. In most cases, national decision-makers do not wish to change this situation.

Circumstances may now be changing, however, and, in some cases, radically. Development paradigms are being reexamined, probably because of negative experiences throughout the world and changes in mainstream culture as a result of the early effects of the information revolution. New and alternative approaches are now being considered, typically under the rubric of "sustainable development."

The information revolution is opening many new channels of communication to local groups in, among other things, the field of environmental management. People are becoming more involved in their communities, better informed about options, and more determined to have a say in their future — be it in devising new development models at the local level, formulating policies on local issues, or advocating decisions at the central level about issues affecting them.

Because of the wide proliferation of more, and more diverse, information, environmental management can no longer be considered the reserve of a few. Now, if authorities want to engage in environmentally unfriendly actions in communities, they must often first convince ombudsmen, local groups, senior citizens, schoolchildren, and women and men of all professions of the positive impact of their projects. In addition, more people are acquiring the means to propose their own solutions, based on both their own traditional and empirical knowledge, which is gradually becoming properly validated, and the scientific and technological knowledge that is becoming increasingly available to all.

Development of global financial markets

Times have changed since wealth was measured in terms of salt, corn, or gold coins. Even paper money is losing value as the nearly 200 million Visa credit cards accepted in 6.5 million stores throughout the world are used to transact about $650 million[2] in business every day (Toffler 1990, p. 61). Including other credit cards, the figure is five times this amount. In addition, a huge number of transactions are carried out using cheques, shares, money orders, and so on. As a result of the information revolution, a growing volume of financial operations is carried out with "electronic money." The trend is clearly toward more widespread substitution of paper-based transactions with electronic operations.

The development of this "virtual" framework has made international monetary systems more volatile; financial and commercial transactions can be carried out at a speed that is changing the rhythm of political and economic events. Financial decisions are made at a moment's notice, at any hour of the day or night. Global markets never close. Effects are almost instantaneous. When a major financial operation takes place or an economic policy announced, repercussions can be felt throughout the world in a matter of minutes.

A further consequence of the information-based management of money has been the internationalization of money markets and a subsequent blurring of financial borders. There are increasing ties between currencies and national governments are experiencing greater difficulty in defining autonomous policies.

Somewhat paradoxically, however, financial trends are developing "on their own." It is becoming increasingly difficult to control markets, as many more people, acting on their own, are making many more decisions over short periods of time. Central banks are having problems ensuring the stability of national currencies or the behaviour of other financial parameters.

This situation is exacerbated by the similarly widespread automation of markets and the development of new, early forecasting programs. There are "a dozen firms...managing more than 100 million dollars [US] each on the basis of advice generated by computers" (*Economist* 1993a, p. 3). Growing numbers of mathematicians and computer experts are dedicated to predicting market trends by computerized nonlinear

---

[2] All dollar values in this book are expressed in US currency.

forecasting and other tools that increase the speed and accuracy of financial decisions. The effects of this practice are not yet wholly understood, but they are already playing a role in the globalization trend and in liberating at least some aspects of the financial market from monopolistic control.

Development of more effective transportation networks

Although to a much lesser degree than the flow of information, the transportation of merchandise has been deeply affected by postindustrial changes. The internationalization of air traffic allows for the rapid transportation of a wide range of lightweight, high-value, perishable, or time-sensitive merchandise, such as electronic equipment and parts, food, flowers, and newsprint. The movement of freight by sea has also become more efficient with the development of computerized shipping

A wide range of industrial merchandise is rapidly reaching formerly isolated areas of the world, such as inner Mongolia.

and the associated improvement of commercial systems, faster ships, and modular packaging. The effectiveness and safety of shipping has been improved considerably by the worldwide adoption of container systems, which reduce the risk of theft and spoilage and significantly accelerate the loading and unloading of goods.

These improvements have promoted the growth of trade worldwide by reducing shipping costs and facilitating redistribution of production. Production occurs more and more often at the most "convenient" place, that is, the most economic, simplest, and safest site available. This is making it more difficult for governments and lobby groups to retain industries or other economic activities artificially in noneconomic situations.

The "lubrication" of merchandise transport systems is also playing a role in the uniformity–diversity dichotomy. On the one hand, there is movement toward uniformity, through stricter and more widespread application of standards, specifications, and quality control. On the other hand, container systems permit the movement of diverse products within a highly standardized system. As with information, the final result will likely display both characteristics.

Movement of people

Another element in this changing world is the increased speed, volume, and accessibility of transportation for people, mainly by air travel. At any moment, throughout the world, several thousand planes are in the air, transporting tens if not hundreds of thousands of people over hundreds or thousands of kilometres. In addition, ground transportation (by automobile, bus, or train) has also become much more flexible, accessible, and rapid, increasing severalfold the number of kilometres that people travel during their lives.

The effects of this increase in travel are felt in many ways. First, there has been phenomenal growth in the tourist industry. Many countries receive over 10 million visitors annually (mainly tourists); in some popular tourist destinations, such as Spain, Italy, the United States, and Mexico, the number of visitors can surpass 30 or 40 million per year. Second, business travel has similarly increased. Business dealings are carried out more frequently and effectively by complementing telecommunications with face-to-face contact. Third, previously difficult international and national social contacts are now becoming commonplace. Thousands of international or interstate sports competitions, conferences, and other events are becoming the rule rather than the exception. Last, but not least, the ease of international travel has increased the flow of international migrants. The main emigration routes, over which people are driven by social, economic, and political situations and events, have been made more accessible by better transportation.

This increase in the transnational flow of people is a major factor in globalization. Visitors interact in many ways with their host countries, exchanging money, purchasing products, influencing (and being influenced by) culture. Migrants interact still more. They affect local job markets, they experience and produce cultural changes, and they mix socially and genetically. The result is an unprecedented mixture of cultures and groups, with the subsequent acquisition or loss of knowledge, changes in outlook, more rapid evolution of processes, behaviour, and attitudes.

Like other global trends, increased travel has produced uniformity, while also fostering diversity. The two processes are taking place simultaneously, although probably at different levels of social systems and consciousness.

Globalization and the unequal distribution of wealth

As described above, globalization is resulting in less differentiation among many aspects of society and life. At the same time, a rebirth of diversification is being promoted by the democratization of information through the expansion of electronic networks and the increasing number of channels of communication. Some important elements in both national and international spheres, however, do not seem to be profiting from either trend. Instead, these processes lead to the unequal distribution of resources, products, and access to money among much of the world's population. International economic disparities do not appear to be decreasing as a result of recent developments; on the contrary, they seem to be growing.

The difference between the real incomes of the poorest and richest people in the world is huge. Annual per-capita income in the 16 richest countries varies from $10 420 to $21 250, averaging about $15 000. At the other extreme, the annual per-capita income in the 25 poorest countries ranges from $80 (Mozambique) to $350 (India), with an average of about $220. Five days' accumulation of per-capita income in the 16 richest countries (total population, 725 million) is equal to 1 year of per-capita income in the 25 poorest (total population, 1 575 million) (WRI 1992).

These figures are averages, however. The income of the poorest people in the poorest countries is considerably lower than the national average. It is estimated to be less than $60 or $80 a year and, in the poorest tenth of the population, probably does not exceed $40. The hourly wage of a well-paid professional in a developed country is often over $100; this can represent 2 or even 3 years' earnings for someone in the poorest sectors of the poorest countries.

Differences in quality of life

Do such quantitative comparisons reflect differences of the same order of magnitude in the quality of life of populations? The answer to this question is as varied as the criteria for evaluating such an elusive concept as quality of life. From one point of view, the quality of life of an itinerant farmer in the highlands of New Guinea may be higher than that of a neurotic Wall Street executive, despite the astronomical difference in income.

The United Nations Development Programme (UNDP) has defined a "human development index" (HDI), which gives a rough idea of the differences in quality of life in the richest and poorest countries of the world (UNDP 1994). The HDI is based on life expectancy, adult literacy, schooling, and income. The maximum value of the HDI is 1.0. UNDP results show 19 countries with an HDI exceeding 0.9; 25 have an HDI below 0.3 (see Table 1 for examples). Although this measure provides only a general idea of quality of life and cannot be assumed to be a mathematical expression, the great variance in HDIs further

Table 1. The human development index (HDI):
10 highest and 10 lowest.

Rank	Country	HDI
1	Canada	0.932
2	Switzerland	0.931
3	Japan	0.929
4	Sweden	0.928
5	Norway	0.928
6	France	0.927
7	Australia	0.926
8	United States	0.925
9	Netherlands	0.923
10	United Kingdom	0.919
164	Djibouti	0.226
165	Guinea-Bissau	0.224
166	Gambia	0.215
167	Mali	0.214
168	Chad	0.212
169	Niger	0.209
170	Sierra Leone	0.209
171	Afghanistan	0.208
172	Burkina Faso	0.203
173	Guinea	0.191

Source: UNDP (1994).

demonstrates the abysmal gap that exists between the richest and poor-est countries in terms of quality of life.

People in developed countries are better fed and live in a healthier, less contaminated environment, with fewer infectious diseases.[3] There-fore, they are sick much less frequently; in addition, these relatively healthy people have easier access to a much more efficient health-care system containing the best human resources, expensive medicine, and sophisticated equipment for diagnosis and treatment of illnesses.

---

[3] This is not always true, however. Some forms of contamination that are not easily detectable are found more frequently in the developed world than in Third World countries, although these examples are becoming less common because of globalization.

The average person in a poor country often works long hours in an unhealthy environment, in a confined space, and in an uncomfortable position; breathes toxic substances; is faced with long trips on crowded buses or trains; and must support a large family on an insufficient salary. In addition, he or she frequently lives in a degraded environment, where there is a high risk of natural catastrophes, such as landslides or floods.

The average person in a rich country has more free time and more options for using it. He or she can take up a sport or other exercise and has access to a range of health products that allow him or her to maintain a healthy life-style. A person in a poor country has little free time; he or she has an unbalanced diet and less resistance to disease. Often, living in high-density areas where appropriate hygiene may be difficult or impossible, the poor are faced with a much higher prevalence of infectious diseases.

To be objective, we must recognize that these situations and evaluations do not apply to all social sectors in rich and poor countries. There are poor sectors in rich countries and very rich sectors in poor countries. The standard of living of the upper classes in some poor countries may seem sumptuous, even compared with that of the average person in developed countries. However, a huge gap exists between the two worlds that appears to be increasing daily.

There are several reasons for the increase. First, the populations of poor countries are growing much faster than those in rich countries, making it increasingly more difficult to provide employment and services for all. Second, the environment of poor countries is being degraded faster and, as a result, their production base is shrinking. Third, poor countries are losing their best human resources to the North. Finally, goods and wealth produced in poor countries are being systematically transferred to the rich through export of capital; payment of royalties, profits, loans, and interest; deterioration of the terms of exchange; and processes of cultural alienation that are promoting unnecessary and frivolous types of consumption, again favouring the transfer of money and resources from the poor to the rich.

In Bombay and many other cities of India, extreme poverty has
resulted in the spread of prostitution and sexually transmitted
diseases, such as AIDS and syphilis.

Effects of international disparities on the environment

The huge differences separating the rich and poor populations of the
world are having an unmistakable effect on the environment at all levels. Poverty is a prime cause of many of the world's serious environmental problems. In most countries, the urban poor must survive in crowded
conditions, without appropriate sanitation and waste-disposal services.
As a result, poor neighbourhoods are becoming a major cause of water
and soil degradation, both in their immediate areas and "downslope" or
downstream. In some countries, landless rural poor are forced to move
into inappropriate locations, cutting and burning trees to clear land for
subsistence farming or raising cattle, or excavating the soil and sediments to extract the minerals that allow them to survive.

A large part of environmental degradation, including desertification, erosion, and contamination processes, is the direct result of the
efforts of poor people to make a living — often, simply to survive. The
issue, however, is not why these people are harming the environment

and how they can change their behaviour; the real issue is why they are in a situation where this is their only recourse.

Not all environmental problems are the result of poverty. Many (perhaps the most acute and wide-ranging problems) result from economic affluence and indiscriminate consumption. Wealthy countries are responsible for burning most of the world's nonrenewable fuel. They produce the largest volumes of solid and liquid wastes, produce enormous volumes of unnatural gaseous emissions, possess the largest depredatory fishing fleets, and consume most of the goods produced in environmentally unfriendly ways in the poorer countries. Finally, through the promotion of export-driven economics in developing countries, the wealthy nations force these countries into positions in which environmental degradation becomes unavoidable.

There is a strong relation between the inequitable social structure of the world and the main processes of environmental degradation that are taking place across the planet. A sustainable approach to environmental management must address the paramount need to restructure the distribution of wealth among countries and among people. Harmonization of production–consumption and the more equitable distribution of wealth are preconditions for sustainable environmental management.

International migration

Differences in quality of life are increasing in an epoch of intense globalization of communications and transport. As a result, for the first time in history, most inhabitants of poorer countries have become aware that people in other places live not only differently, but much better.

Third World people, representing 80% of the world's population, increasingly want to emigrate to the developed world. Salvadoreans, Nicaraguans, Peruvians, and many other Latin American people dream of emigrating to the United States and Canada. Thousands of North Africans would like to move to France, Belgium, and Switzerland. Many Indians and Pakistanis would like to emigrate to Britain or Saudi Arabia.

Each year, several million people attempt to fulfill this wish, and a considerable number succeed. They use the most varied and imaginative methods. Some cross a desert or river; others cross larger bodies of water in small boats. Still others try their luck by legal means, hoping to be included in the quotas of Canada or the United States, or through agreements between governments. Professional people and entrepreneurs have an advantage. Those who possess special expertise or belong to the qualified professions are accepted with relative ease.

One result of these migratory fluxes is the development of stricter policies and strategies by the rich countries to prevent uncontrolled arrivals. Careful controls, visa requirements, and financial guarantees are all geared toward closing borders. Despite these measures, however, migratory pressure is so great that large numbers manage to squeeze through or around the various "filters," and settle in the targeted countries where their situation is often secured after several years through one of the periodic amnesties, which, in a way, are a recognition of the impotence of the police and immigration systems in preventing people from escaping living conditions in the South.

Currently, the main recipient countries for immigrants are the largest and least densely populated: the United States, Canada, and Australia. These three countries absorb about 1.5 million immigrants every year, that is, approximately half of the total migration to developed countries.

Immigration to the United States

The United States alone receives more than 1 million immigrants a year. California, the richest and most populated state in the country, increased its population from less than 26 million in 1980 to the current 31.5 million. Foreign immigration accounted for about 40% of the increase (Appleby 1993). In the area of San Diego alone, legal immigrants constitute more than half the population, and it is estimated that there are 200 thousand illegal immigrants in the population of 2 million. Similar situations are found in other southern US cities, such as Houston, Los Angeles, and San Antonio.

A significant segment of the immigrant population ends up in the sector of American society living in poverty.[4] The shantytowns of San Diego are typical poor neighbourhoods, composed of recent, mainly illegal immigrants. The Los Diablos slum in San Diego County is "a wasteland of rusting cars and makeshift housing, an acreage owned by the city and squatted on for many years" (Appleby 1993). These squatters work at small construction projects or pick tomatoes and cucumbers for below-minimum wages; they earn about $3 per hour, compared with the minimum wage of $4.50 per hour (in Mexico, however, the same work pays one-tenth that amount). Squatter camps like Los Diablos can be found throughout southern California, Arizona, New Mexico, Texas, and Florida in the inner cities or suburbs of many large metropolitan areas. In some ways, they represent the Third World inside the developed world.

In 1992, over 1 million people immigrated to the United States, of which 841 thousand were classified as "legal" (*Business Week* 1992). Almost half were from Latin America, with 23% coming from Mexico, the country "sending" the most migrants to its northern neighbours. Of the remainder, 13.1% came from the Caribbean and 11.1% came from Central and South America.

More than a third (35.2%) of the remaining legal immigrants came from Asia. During recent years there has been an increase in immigration from eastern Europe, which previously had not exceeded 8%, and a relatively small amount of immigration from Africa (about 2%).

These legal immigrants include a considerable number of people with high levels of education: 26.6% have university degrees, although in their own countries people with degrees make up only a small percentage of the population. This phenomenon has been referred to as the "brain drain." It tends to accentuate North–South disparities, strengthening human resources in countries with well-developed capacities and reducing the already weak professional base of poorer countries. The countries of origin of migrants with the highest education are India

---

[4] Most of the poor in the country are born in the United States, usually as members of ethnic minorities (Afro-Americans, Hispanic-Americans, and American Indians).

(average schooling, 15 years), Philippines (14 years), and Korea (13 years). The lowest level of education is found in Mexican immigrants (7 years).

Not only do these immigrants possess relatively high levels of education, they are also often trained and experienced in highly specialized occupations. For example, 40% of AT&T's researchers were born outside the United States (*Business Week* 1992). A similar proportion of the professionals in the Silicon Valley are also immigrants. According to *Business Week*, the next generation of engineers in highly sophisticated US companies will be dominated by immigrants.

While these immigration trends continue, there is evidence of a change in the types of jobs available in the United States. As the country moves toward a postindustrial, third-wave society and redistribution of its global productive roles, a large number of labour-intensive production activities are being transferred to less-developed countries like Mexico. Many jobs that were once performed by immigrants or unspecialized American workers have disappeared, a situation that is affecting the segment of the American work force that depends on these jobs for its survival.

One frequently hears that it is the continuous influx of immigrants that is creating job scarcity. Although research has shown that immigrants create more jobs than they take, their presence can contribute to the level of frustration in society. There is widespread feeling among American citizens that, to solve the unemployment problem, immigration must be stopped or drastically reduced. In some areas, however, the lack of inexpensive immigrant labour may promote the transfer of many jobs to sites in Brazil, Guatemala, Mexico, or other countries, including some jobs now performed by American workers.

Immigration to other developed countries

The population density in Canada and Australia is less than 3 people per square kilometre. Immigration to Canada has ranged from 100 to 200 thousand people a year over the last few years. Australia has accepted slightly fewer people than Canada.

Lately, a large proportion of Canadian immigrants have come from Asia (especially those in Vancouver, Toronto, and other large cities), eastern Europe, and, to a lesser degree, the Middle East and Latin America. As a result of the recent war in Somalia, many citizens from this country have also come to Canada, many of them as refugees.

In Australia, the immigrant population includes a considerable number of people from neighbouring Far Eastern countries (China, India, Indonesia, Melanesia, Pakistan, the Philippines, Polynesia, and Vietnam), as well as eastern Europe.

In Europe, immigration patterns are closely related to the affiliations of former Third World colonies. France and Belgium have received many immigrants from the Francophone countries of Africa (Algeria, Morocco, and Tunisia); the United Kingdom is the destination of Indians and Pakistanis; Holland of Indonesians; Portugal of people from Angola, Cape Verde Islands, Guinea, and Mozambique; and Spain of Spanish-Americans, Moroccans, and other Africans.

The southern coast of Spain, in Andalucía near Tarifa, is the destination of tens of thousands of illegal immigrants who cross the Strait of Gibraltar in *pateras*. Moroccans, Mauritanians, Senegalese, and other Africans from south of the Sahara cross the strait with the help of *pasadores* or *lobos*. Once they reach Spain, some manage to move into other countries, such as France and Germany, but many remain on the Iberian Peninsula.

In Europe, African and Asian workers are a source of inexpensive labour for jobs not attractive to nationals. As a result, it has become increasingly difficult for some of the richer European countries to do without their work. In addition to the large number of immigrants with low professional qualifications, Europe receives a significant number of immigrants with higher qualifications (generally through legal or semi-legal channels), arriving as students, invited professors, professionals, and qualified technicians.

A portion of the earnings of immigrants is transferred to their countries of origin. For example, it is estimated that Morocco receives over $1 billion as a result of these remittances (*El País* 1992). Similar figures have been reported for Algeria, Tunisia, and, to a lesser degree, sub-Saharan countries.

As in North America, a significant sector of the immigrant population has a high level of education, strengthening the knowledge base of European countries, while reducing such resources in the countries of origin. Third World countries spend their limited financial resources training their professionals, only to have the few well-trained people who complete their studies quickly absorbed by the much richer North.

The development of free markets

Immediately after the Second World War, the main political powers began negotiations to reduce tariffs and duties worldwide, giving birth to GATT (the General Agreement on Tariffs and Trade). With the participation of 23 countries, this agreement was concluded in Geneva, Switzerland, in 1947, and took effect in 1948.

At that time, the objective was to approve an interim agreement until an international agency could assume responsibility for coordination and management of international trade relations. However, such an agency was never formed and GATT remains the principal tool for liberalizing world trade. Since its inception, GATT has expanded to include more than 100 countries by the early 1990s.

An attempt to liberalize regional trade took place in western Europe after 1958 when the European Common Market was formed by Belgium, France, Germany, Italy, Luxembourg, and the Netherlands. This trading bloc, now know as the European Community (EC), grew further to include Denmark, Ireland, and the United Kingdom (1973), Greece (1981), and Spain and Portugal (1986). By 1993, other European countries were negotiating entry and, before the end of the century, it is likely that the remaining Scandinavian countries (Finland, Norway, and Sweden) and Austria will join. The Czech Republic, Estonia, Hungary, Latvia, Lithuania, Malta, Poland, and Slovenia are also interested, although their incorporation will probably not occur before the year 2000.

The EC countries trade mainly with their economic partners (78% of the Netherlands' exports remain in the EC; Belgium and

Luxembourg, 75%; Ireland, 75%; Portugal, 74%; Spain, 71%; France, 62%; Italy, 59%; United Kingdom, 55%; Germany, 53%). Most of the remaining commerce is directed to North America and the Far East. The role of Third World countries in European commerce is less important.

Starting in 1988, a second major commercial bloc was formed in North America when the United States and Canada negotiated a free trade agreement. In 1993, an agreement was reached between these two countries and Mexico to ensure its integration into the process through the North American Free Trade Agreement (NAFTA). The formalization of this treaty has generated strong opposition from some sectors of both the Canadian and the American public who believe that opening the borders will release a flood of companies moving south to Mexico in search of a less-expensive environment, while posing the risk of increased immigration to the United States and Canada.

A recent article (*Economist* 1993b) expressed the view of many who think that there may be exactly the opposite effect. It cites the case of a General Motors plant planning to move a large portion of the production of Cavalier vehicles from Ramos Arizpe, Mexico, to Lansing, Michigan. According to the article, Mexican labour costs are only 35% lower than those in the United States and 40% lower than Canada's, when average wages are adjusted for benefits and lower productivity. The effect of NAFTA may thus be less pronounced than feared by those who oppose it.

Following a proposal of then President of the United States, George Bush (the 1990 "Initiative for the Americas"), other Latin American countries are also making progress toward similar agreements. The most important regional block is the MERCOSUR, comprising Argentina, Brazil, Paraguay, and Uruguay, complemented by the Central American Free Market (Costa Rica, Guatemala, Honduras, Nicaragua, and El Salvador) and the Andean Group (Bolivia, Colombia, Ecuador, and Venezuela). Chile and Peru have not joined any of these liberalization initiatives.

Since the 1960s, attempts have been made to create a Latin American free market — after the formation of the Asociación

Latino-Americana de Libre Comercio, which became Asociación Latino-Americana de Integration (ALADI) after the treaty of Montevideo. ALADI's role has been mainly to provide an institutional framework for regional agreements dealing with integration processes, including trade liberalization.

Recent GATT negotiations took place in this environment of globalization. Many difficulties were encountered during the "Uruguay round," particularly because of the insistence of some EC countries on maintaining certain farming subsidies. The document resulting from the Uruguay round of GATT was approved and signed by the 117 member countries on 15 December 1993 in Geneva, Switzerland. Although the final agreement was not as wide ranging as expected, tariffs will decrease by an average 40%. The relatively successful conclusion of this agreement shows that the world continues to move toward globalization and that, although international commerce is complex, the barriers that used to prevent the development of open trade relations are gradually being dismantled.

Complexities of international commerce and their effects on globalization

Evidence from recent history shows that globalization processes are unstoppable because they tend to feed on each other. Current globalization trends are based on a framework of unidirectional openings (liberal approaches in developing countries, continued protectionism in developed economies). It is an internationalization controlled from the financial decision-making centres in the North.

Farming systems in the United States and the EC remain supported by direct and indirect subsidies. In Europe, this is viewed by some as overt protectionism; in the United States, the subsidies are more indirect — for example, subsidized water for irrigated agriculture in California and other western states.

Third World countries, on the other hand, pressured by the need to service large debts and conditioned by liberalizing programs imposed by the International Monetary Fund (IMF) and other lending agencies, have been drawn into export-promotion campaigns. These have forced them to accept unfavourable terms of exchange because of import quotas, used as instruments of political pressure, or in relation to refinancing their foreign debt.

The desperate need to export, coupled with the necessity of creating new sources of employment, has compelled many developing countries to be less selective in their acceptance of new industries transferred from developed countries, including the rapidly spreading *maquiladoras*, which generally use production systems that are not only highly exploitive of the work force, detrimental to health, and environmentally unfriendly, but also teach workers almost nothing that can be applied elsewhere (see Chapter 11 for a detailed description).

Economic globalization and environmental degradation

Economic globalization and liberalization of trade are having a strong impact on the environment at local, regional, and global levels. Whenever trade barriers are lowered or eliminated, many economic activities that had previously been carried out under their protection also tend to disappear, often to relocate in other areas where economic survival is easier.

Generally, the dominant factor in competitive production is cost. Developed countries must compensate for their high labour, tax, and environmental costs through more productive technologies, higher production levels, and more efficient management strategies. Despite the high costs, there are clear advantages to producing certain goods in developed countries: well-organized and efficient infrastructures, high capacity of existing human resources, better quality control, and proximity to markets. However, a number of productive activities in developed countries would not be able to survive for long without the shields of protectionist trade barriers and subsidies.

Because globalization processes tend to remove these barriers, many productive activities traditionally associated with developed economies are gradually being transferred to developing countries. In some cases, this happens through partial transfer of some operations in the productive chain, such as assembly or production of parts for industrial use. Such transferred operations can be carried out at a lower cost at the receiving site because of lower labour and environmental costs.

Normally, this transfer involves agreements between the countries to allow productive complementarity. In most cases, the transferring country charges duty only on the value added in the host country, and the host country opens "free zones" to allow entry and exit of raw materials and merchandise with minimal or no import–export duty. These industries are called *maquiladoras* and are common in Costa Rica, the Dominican Republic, Guatemala, Mexico, and, with slight modifications, in some countries of East Asia and North Africa.

Often, when the whole economic activity becomes uneconomical in the developed country, the entire productive process can be transferred to the partner country. Many metallurgical, textile, and electronics industries, among others, have been transferred in this way. Similar arrangements are being made in relation to agricultural activities (some Californian crops have been transferred to Brazil, Chile, and Mexico), forestry (the Canadian forest industry is having trouble competing with counterparts in Brazil and Chile), and aquaculture (shrimp farms have been established in Ecuador and the Philippines).

This global restructuring of production is having a profound effect on the environment. Most of the industries or activities moving to developing countries have some potential for environmental degradation. A considerable number of them produce toxic wastes or emissions that can introduce negative elements into water, air, or soils. When these industries or activities are located in developed countries, a long social learning process has contributed to the development of a set of environmental laws to address, more or less efficiently, their potentially hazardous effects. Developed countries have preventive and reactive systems, including technical solutions to environmental degradation, policies and rules for that purpose, definitions of responsibility and accountability, and appropriate institutions, to deal with environmental problems. Many developing countries lack these systems. Some laws may exist, but they are poorly applied (if at all). Recently, progress has been made in several countries, but it is insufficient to prevent serious environmental degradation.

Thus, the restructuring of production appears to be threatening the environment at local, national, regional, and global levels. For example, acid rain, which was once common only in northeastern North America and western Europe, has become a serious issue in several Third World countries, including Brazil, China, and India. Industrial procedures to check environmental degradation are often bypassed as industries relocate to Third World countries where such requirements do not apply or can be circumvented. New irrigated-farming projects in developing countries are using water at a rate well above the renewability potential of aquifers or surface water bodies. Farming and neo-forestry activities are being carried out on land from which rich and diverse native forests have been eliminated.

The balance is systematically negative: less care is exercised or responsibility taken; fewer resources are applied to environmental protection; soil is eroded; aquifers, streams, lakes, and coastal waters are contaminated; forests are disappearing; exotic species are introduced without consideration of their ecological effects; and the atmosphere is polluted. Any long-term approach to environmentally sustainable development must consider these effects of globalization. The problems must be addressed before they become impossible or too expensive to reverse.

3

Planet-wide Deterioration

....

People know that their actions can have considerable effect on local environments. When a campfire is lit, hundreds of hectares of forest may disappear in flames. Building a dam can flood an extensive low-lying area. Cities affect the local climate, increasing average temperatures and changing other characteristics of the overlying atmosphere. Large lakes can be rendered lifeless by contaminants discharged into them.

On a regional scale, it is not as easy to recognize environmental changes caused by human activities. However, it is now becoming clear that whole regions downwind of large industrial areas are being strongly affected by acid rain, that some species have disappeared from fishing regions, and that overgrazing or deforestation is affecting the regional climates of the Sahel and Amazon.

It is even more difficult to imagine the effects of anthropogenic action on the global environment. The Earth is so large and the atmosphere so extensive that past experience suggests that human activities will never reach the dimension necessary to produce changes on a planetary scale. Today, however, changes are occurring at an almost exponential rate, and many past theories may no longer apply.

Our sister planet

As the Earth moves around the sun, it is accompanied by the Moon. Before the 1960s, humans had no influence on the lunar environment. For 4 billion years or more, our sister planet evolved according to the general laws of celestial physics, its surface modified only by lava flows (in very ancient times), meteorite impacts, terrestrial tides, and solar radiation and particles.

For many years, even during the lunar landings of the late 1960s and early 1970s, it was believed that the Moon had no atmosphere. Now we know that it possesses a very thin one, consisting mainly of helium, argon, sodium, potassium, radon, and polonium (data from the 1972 Lunar Atmospheric Composition Experiment, see Stern 1993). The total mass of the lunar atmosphere is small — only about 30 tonnes for the whole planet.

The effect of the Apollo missions on the lunar environment was considerable. Each flight increased the mass of the lunar atmosphere by one-third. The gas escaped after a few weeks, but it was "renewed" during each mission. The impact of establishing a settlement on the Moon would be enormous. The Moon missions showed that humans can change planets, even without meaning to.

The Earth is much bigger than the Moon: its diameter is four times greater and it is some 90 times more massive. Every day, however, the equivalent of several hundred thousand "Apollo missions" take place as aircraft take off and land. In addition, 500 million cars and 10 million factories use atmospheric gases and release others in ways quite contrary to natural cycles.

The production of carbon dioxide (CO_2), for example, has been increasing exponentially since the beginning of the industrial revolution. During the first stages of the industrial era, coal was burned in large quantities. Later, factories turned to petroleum, which is still used, and the volume of CO_2 and other associated gases being emitted into the air is steadily increasing.

How much can the atmosphere of a planet like Earth absorb before changes start to occur in the gaseous layers and the crust? We don't know the answer. Changes may already have started, and the situation may already be critical. We are "playing with fire" in both the literal and symbolic sense. We have good reason to worry, mainly because we still know so little. In the following section, some factors that might allow us to decipher the indicators of global change are discussed.

The unusual, oxygenated planet

Among the planets of the solar system, the Earth is an oddity. Although several bodies are similar in volume and mass (Venus, Mars, Mercury, Ganymede, and Titan), several features of the Earth make it unique. The Earth is the only known planet with a large oceanic area; its atmosphere contains very little CO_2 (about 0.3%) and a large amount of free oxygen (21%).

The level of oxygen seems particularly high when we consider that it is a very active gas and combines with many other elements. It is found on many other planets, but usually combined with carbon or hydrogen as CO_2 and water (in gaseous or solid forms) or with silicon, aluminium, and other elements to form the crystal lattices of minerals. Free oxygen does not exist in significant quantities on any other planet.

On Earth, oxygen occurs in water, ice, and rocks. In fact, oxygen represents 45% of the total mass of the Earth's crust and 90% of the total volume. However, the huge amount of free oxygen in the atmosphere is unique in the solar system, and this oxygen has existed for many hundred million years. There is every indication that its proportion has increased during geological time, as a result of a long period of photosynthetic activity by algae and green plants.

Originally, Earth was probably more like Venus and Mars. Venus' atmosphere is composed mainly of CO_2 (95%) and nitrogen (4%); the Martian atmosphere is 94% CO_2 and 5% nitrogen. Three billion years ago, the amount of CO_2 in the Earth's atmosphere was also high (perhaps over 90%); however, photosynthetic activity released the oxygen from CO_2 to form organic matter. It is believed that noticeable volumes of free oxygen first appeared about 2 billion years ago. One billion years later, it probably made up 1 to 3% of the atmosphere and ozone started filtering out ultraviolet radiation. The 5% level was probably reached about 750 million years ago, and the current oxygen concentration was not reached until about 100 million years ago (Cloud and Gibor 1970). A large proportion of the carbon was buried in sediments as limestone, coal, petroleum, and gas. A small amount remained in the atmosphere or dissolved in ocean waters.

While the level of CO_2 decreased and carbon was trapped in geological layers, oxygen molecules were being released into the atmosphere, increasing slowly to a concentration of about 20%. The upper limit for oxygen concentration is related to the probability of natural fires occurring; the more free oxygen there is, the more likely spontaneous fires will break out. Fires oxidize the carbon in the organic matter, such as wood, to produce CO_2, thus reducing the amount of oxygen in the air relative to CO_2.

The decrease in CO_2 concentration during geological times brought about important climatic changes, the main one likely being a decrease in average temperature. Carbon dioxide in the atmosphere produces a strong greenhouse effect, and its elimination promotes a general cooling of the atmosphere. The decrease in CO_2 was not continuous. It occurred in leaps, and qualitative changes were determined by the development of new, more sophisticated biological systems to use it.

According to Lovelock (1988, p. 164), the decrease in CO_2 was also a way for the planet to cool in spite of increasing solar heat.[5] In other words, life seems to possess a "thermostat" that has ensured a relatively constant temperature throughout geological times, a temperature that allows survival of life. Every time the solar heat increased to a certain level, new biological systems developed to use smaller proportions of CO_2, causing the concentration of this gas to decrease further, cooling the biosphere.

Through successive adaptations of photosynthetic processes, biosystems were able to reduce the CO_2 content in the air to 0.3%, the current level. If solar radiation continues to increase, there is little room for additional cooling (that is, for continued lowering of CO_2 levels). In that respect, biological systems are "living on the edge." If additional

---

[5] It is uncertain if the sun's radiation increased during geological times, but an augmentation of the heat received by the Earth would explain some curious characteristics of the chemical evolution of the atmosphere.

CO_2 is released into the air, and if the volume and activity of CO_2 users (algae and plants) are reduced because of deforestation and water pollution by pesticides and oil, there is a risk that the thermostat may break down (Cloud and Gibor 1970). When that happens, it may be too late to change course.

We must seriously consider a rapid, drastic reduction in systems that burn fossil fuels and produce large quantities of CO_2 and other greenhouse gases. Postponing action will put at risk not only the survival of humankind, but that of "Gaia" itself.

The paradox of ozone

Ozone can be a problem gas: in the lower atmosphere, there may be too much of it and it is an indicator of pollution; in the upper atmosphere, there is not enough to block undesirable solar radiation. In both cases, the problem results from anthropogenic contamination of the air.

Oxygen is a basic building block of our planet. The crust, the oceans, and the atmosphere all contain important proportions of oxygen. Free oxygen, which is only present in the atmosphere, occurs as the diatomic molecule O_2. In some cases, as a result of various natural or artificial causes, oxygen may occur as a triatomic molecule or ozone (O_3).

When normal diatomic oxygen molecules reach the stratosphere, they are exposed to high-energy ultraviolet radiation, resulting in the formation of ozone. Ozone in the stratosphere filters out an important part of the ultraviolet solar spectrum. Without this protective layer, the amount of ultraviolet radiation reaching the Earth's surface would increase to the detriment of all living organisms, including humans. The main effects would be at the molecular level, resulting in genetic malformations, cancers, and other diseases.

The concentration of ozone in the stratosphere has been gradually decreasing (despite seasonal variations), particularly over both polar regions. In Antarctica, where the process has received more attention, an "ozone hole" was observed in the early 1980s. More recently, an "Arctic hole" has also been found. In other parts of the ozone layer, there is also widespread thinning, which is becoming significant enough to affect biological activities.

The culprits identified as being responsible for this change are the chlorofluorocarbons (CFC-11 and CFC-12) contained in aerosol sprays, refrigerants, solvents, and foams. About 1 million tonnes of CFCs are emitted into the air every year. They remain in the atmosphere for 60 to 100 years — the current atmospheric concentration of chlorine is about 3 parts per billion (ppb) (Graedel and Crutzen 1989).

In the early 1970s, it was already possible to detect CFCs in Antarctica (Lovelock 1988). At that time, the concentration in the southern hemisphere was about 40 parts per trillion (ppt) and 50 to 70 ppt in the northern hemisphere. The threat to the ozone layer was not yet recognized. In 1974, Rowland and Molina (see Lovelock 1988) developed the hypothesis that CFCs were a source of chlorine and, therefore, a threat to the ozone layer. Since then, considerable scientific research has been done and, although not unanimously, it is generally believed that CFCs are indeed having deleterious effects on the ozone layer.

At ground level, ozone is a secondary photochemical oxidant, which is formed as a result of various human activities, including automobile engine combustion. Although it is not part of the emissions themselves, ozone is formed as an immediate result and is an important component of smog. Contamination in urban and industrial areas can be measured in terms of "ozone concentrations." The gas is a clear indicator of air quality: the more ozone occurring in the lower atmospheric layers, the more contaminated the air. An improvement in air quality in large metropolitan areas will be accompanied by a reduction in the concentration of ozone. Ozone, itself, at low concentrations, is not a toxic gas, but its presence reveals that pollution emissions are taking place.

Oceans can be degraded too

Oceans and large bodies of water are also being degraded by human activities. Although oceans are very large, occupying nearly three quarters of the Earth's surface, the continuous outflow of untreated effluents into the sea has had persistent and increasing effects, particularly along the shores. Sediment accumulations have increased at the outlets of several large rivers, "plumes" of industrial and urban pollutants are flowing into many coastal areas, and overfishing has had a profound negative effect on marine ecosystems. Thin films of petroleum, foam from detergents, and various floating wastes can be found even far from populated areas. The degradation of oceanic basins has become a planetary phenomenon.

The rivers are becoming muddy

Some time ago, Erhart (1968), traveling by ship along the Congo and Amazon rivers, was puzzled by the lack of turbidity in the water — no sediments, no clays, nothing of the brown colour that one expects of mighty rivers draining such large basins. Eventually, he realized that the clear water was natural. These large streams flowed from rain-forest basins, where there was no erosion. Chemical processes of organic origin predominated. Although the water in these rivers was carrying salts, resulting from the leaching of ions from the soils they drained, no sediments were being transported. Ions of calcium, sodium, potassium, magnesium, and silicon and carbonates, phosphates, and chlorides were carried in the water in small proportions, producing a gradual increase in the salinity of the sea and supplying raw materials for the shells of sea organisms.

Erhart also realized that the old processes of soil formation (weathering) in rain-forest environments were the origin of limestone. Today's calcareous mud at the bottom of the ocean is the current equivalent of the ancient limestones formed (by biostasy) 100 or 200 million years ago during the Mesozoic era, when dinosaurs roamed the Earth. However, the calcareous muds of the past were buried by younger sediments, composed of claystones, siltstones, and associated sandstones (what geologists call "flysch"), during a drier period that followed the humid period that produced the limestones. Erhart concluded that the forest had disappeared and that subsequently the soils had been eroded; he called this situation, in which mechanical processes predominated, rhexistasy.

Today, large forests are disappearing even faster as a result of human action. Deforestation is widespread. Forests are logged or burned, leading to soil erosion; rivers are becoming filled with muddy sediments. Flying over the Amazon brings new surprises every year: its tributaries are becoming yellow or brown in colour; the Amazon itself is no longer dark green; and in geological terms, the forest is starting to die.

In ancient times, forests would die, but others were born. There were always sufficient trees to maintain a low level of CO_2. Now, as all forests are being cut back at the same time, we suspect there is considerable risk to the planet's dynamics.

Overshooting

It is difficult to predict the outcome of current changes. Exponential growth of some components (such as world population) or some factors (temperature of the oceans, level of CO_2) indicates the direction of change, but cannot provide sufficient information to allow us to guess the future of the Gaia system. The Earth is an extremely complex environment, and growth curves are crude instruments for understanding it. In reality, we do not know where or when "overshooting" of limits will take place. At best, these tools give us a slight indication of the risk.

We must remember that natural processes never follow a linear or exponential path indefinitely. Once they reach a ceiling, a change takes place, and new relationships are established. Sometimes factors that are overlooked may be increasing or decreasing exponentially, and their effects may be felt suddenly. The greenhouse effect produces an increase in temperature, which in turn increases evaporation; this leads to increased cloudiness and an increase in the albedo of the planet, reducing radiation and decreasing temperature. Even a relatively simple model like this can be difficult to quantify, however, mainly because the data and relationships are poorly understood. For example, if we introduce the role of algae and photosynthesis in the upper layer of the oceans or the effect of ice melting at the poles, the situation becomes more complex. A model of the planet requires understanding and measuring thousands of variables, some of which are biological or anthropogenic in nature.

Although much can be done toward solving the riddle of our environmental future, we must remain cautious about forecasts. Because so little is known and the risk is so great, survival strategies must rely on the best interpretation of existing data. We may, in the end, "go beyond the limits inadvertently" because of inattention, inadequate information, a slow response, or simply the momentum (Meadows et al. 1992). On this "spaceship Earth," however, we cannot afford to risk overshooting the limits, whatever they may be; we may not have a second chance.

4

Forests under Attack

Management of forest ecosystems has always been one of the most difficult challenges presented to humans. During the agricultural revolution,
societies inhabiting forest areas in Europe, the Middle East, and other
parts of the world started clearing trees to prepare land for crop production. In Roman times, hundreds of thousands of square kilometres of
Mediterranean forests with their deep and fertile soils were eliminated
to make way for cereal crops, such as wheat and barley. In Sudanese
Africa, during the first centuries of the Christian era, a considerable
portion of forest gave way to locally domesticated sorghum and millet
crops and itinerant cattle-raising. In America, many of the forests surrounding the valley of Mexico were gradually removed to make room
for corn and bean farms. In Asia, rice paddies replaced the extensive
forests of China, Indochina, and some of the largest Indonesian islands.

Despite this worldwide reduction in area, at the time of the industrial revolution forests still occupied nearly 30% of the continental
landmass, typically concentrated in humid and subhumid areas. In the
1600s, more than half of Europe and more than 90% of the humid
regions of North and South America were covered by trees. In Africa,
although long-term human habitation had significantly reduced forest

areas (mainly through burning), resulting in "savannization," large tracts of land in humid and subhumid regions remained covered by forests.

In Europe, the industrial revolution brought about systematic and intense degradation of the forests. The main causes were the increase in population and the burning of firewood by industries and individuals. During the 18th and 19th centuries, new villages were established in less productive environments, such as steep and stony slopes in the cooler mountain highlands of the Alps, the Massif Central of France, and the Apennines in Italy; these areas were slowly converted to agricultural production, significantly reducing the forest cover.

In many areas of Europe, population growth outpaced the opening of new farmland. Often, this was simply because land was not available. In many cases, however, it was due to a concentration of land ownership in the hands of a few people. At the beginning of the industrial revolution, most of the surplus rural population had moved to cities to work in the new industries. However, European industries soon proved insufficient to absorb all the migrants. This prompted the migration to America, which by the end of the 19th century and the first half of the 20th century became intensive.

In North America, the arrival of millions of Europeans meant the opening of new forestlands for farming. New England was completely covered by forests in 1620 and largely deforested 150 years later. In the 18th century, more than 4 million hectares of Arkansas marsh and swamp forests were converted to farmland (Reisner 1986). Between 1848 and 1858, Minnesota's population, next to the Canadian border, increased from 10 to 150 thousand (it was promoted from a territory to a state at this time). A similar situation occurred in the 1870s in the territory of Dakota (*National Geographic* 1986). By the late 1870s, more than half the temperate forests of North America had been eliminated, and the process continued for many decades. Because land had become scarce in the east, most new arrivals and many older settlers or their descendants moved west, clearing new land for agriculture.

In South America, most forested areas were in the tropics, particularly in the Amazon basin and the upper basins of the Paraná and

Orinoco rivers. Early deforestation of tropical ecosystems occurred during the colonization period along the northeastern coast of Brazil to make way for sugarcane plantations and, later, by the end of the 19th century, around São Paulo for coffee production.

The deforestation of mountain areas, which had begun in precolonial times, continued after European colonization, reducing forested areas to only the steeper or cooler slopes by the end of the 19th century. Well into the 20th century, however, a considerable portion of the continent's extensive tropical forests remained virtually untouched. This delay in deforestation was probably due to the abundance of grasslands in the more productive temperate areas (the pampas). The only forested areas in temperate climates were on the slopes and narrow plains along the Pacific coast in central and southern Chile and in the highlands of the Planalto of southern Brazil.

Deforestation in the 20th century

In this century, deforestation processes in Latin America have proceeded at a much faster rate. By the 1970s, most of the *Araucaria* forests of the Planalto in Brazil and the forests of the western foothills of the Amazon basin from Colombia to Bolivia had been partially or totally eliminated. More recently, new forest areas have been logged or burned in eastern Paraguay, Mato Grosso in Brazil, and Santa Cruz in Bolivia to make room for cattle and soybean and rice plantations. For the last decade, deforestation in the Brazilian Amazon region has been occurring at the rate of about 21 thousand square kilometres every year (Fearnside et al. 1990), bringing the total area cleared to more than half a million square kilometres in the last two centuries.

In Africa, deforestation activity was widespread, particularly along the Guinean coast, to make way for peanut, cocoa, coconut, and banana plantations. Other areas affected included the central highlands (from Rwanda and Burundi to Uganda) and the tropical forests of south-central Africa from Angola to southern Tanzania. Today, African rain forests are greatly reduced to less than 1 million square kilometres, barely 4% of the total area of the continent and less than 20% of their original area.

In Mali, the use of wood for firewood, charcoal, and construction has resulted in deforestation. Annual wood use in this region is estimated at about 300 kilograms per person (360 kilograms in urban areas and 270 kilograms in rural areas) for a total of 1.7 million tonnes per year. Of this amount, more than 200 thousand tonnes per year are used in the Bamako metropolitan area, which has resulted in the forest retreating toward the southern part of the country. In the Mopti region, the burning of wood to smoke fish is also contributing to rapid deforestation and environmental degradation. Although some reforestation projects have been carried out (often giving priority to exotic instead of more appropriate indigenous trees), the general trend has clearly been toward deforestation. In Sudan, more than 48 million cubic metres of wood is cut every year for charcoal production or for use as fuel.

Deforestation has also been intense in southern and Southeast Asia. The trend has accelerated during the last few decades, particularly in Indonesia and Malaysia, where large, previously untouched areas of Sumatra, Borneo, New Guinea, and the Malaccan Peninsula have suffered extensive forest degradation.

The increasing demand for timber during the first half of the 20th century was met by a resource base mainly composed of natural or semi-natural forests (see Perez Arrarte 1993). During this period, the value of a forest was related to its logging potential. Over the last few decades, however, new potential values of forests have been emphasized: as eco-touristic resources, as sources of biodiversity, etc. This change in attitude has promoted a different approach to forest management and exploitation. Native people in Canada and the United States, who are reluctant to allow logging on their traditional lands, have found important allies in many environmental groups. Pro-logging lobbies are losing their influence, and exploitation of temperate forests in North America and Scandinavia is becoming more difficult.

Besides being "politically incorrect," logging in the North is also becoming uneconomic. In temperate climates, trees grow very slowly. In many areas downwind of industrial centres, wood stands are being affected by acid rain, further complicating things for forestry companies in the northern countries. Profitability among Canadian lumber

In Mali, the removal of wood for fuel or charcoal production is the main cause of deforestation (piles of firewood for sale north of Bamako).

companies decreased substantially from 1990 to 1993. The growth of a strong paper-recycling industry is also affecting the forest business, accelerating this trend. These tendencies have resulted in a decrease in the production of timber and paper pulp from northern forests and a substitution of material from more competitive artificial plantations in warmer latitudes, such as the southern United States, Brazil, Chile, and Argentina.

In many Third World countries, natural forests have also been beset by continuous logging, without allowing time for regeneration. As a result, the amount of material coming from natural tropical forests in these areas has also decreased. In some cases, new artificial forests were planted in place of the natural forests (southern Chile and Misiones in Argentina). In most cases, the newly planted areas are monospecific plantations of exotic trees. In some areas, cleared land has been converted to agriculture or animal production.

Globalization processes are promoting the gradual substitution of natural forests by artificial systems. The redistribution of economic roles is having an effect on the forestry industry at all levels. Some countries that were traditional producers are withdrawing from the international scene, while others that have not been producers are increasing their exports.

These trends are taking place at a time when the demand for timber and paper pulp is increasing worldwide. In spite of this, increased production — from 2.7 billion cubic metres in 1977 to 3.4 billion in 1988 — has been sufficient to meet the demand. Particularly important was the increase in paper pulp production (about 30% for the same period), which appears to be related to the increasing worldwide consumption of paper promoted by the information revolution. Wood and charcoal production increased 33% between 1977 and 1988 (Perez Arrarte 1993, p. 15).

Rain-forest environments

Tropical rain forests are located in areas where steady high temperatures and an abundance of water allow continuous growth of vegetation. Tropical rain forests grow year-round. Average daily temperatures remain between 20° and about 30°C and water shortages are infrequent. In addition, solar radiation is high, further favouring photosynthesis and associated biological processes.

These environments are characterized by multilayered vegetation reaching maximum heights of 40 to 60 metres. Nutrients are mainly stored in living biomass, rather than in the soil. Because of this, when vegetation is removed, the chances of the system recovering to its former state are limited. In addition, microclimatic changes — such as decreasing humidity, increasing temperature, and wind variations — can produce dramatic effects and make germination or regeneration of most native plant species difficult or impossible. Soil erosion, which is negligible under forest cover, increases radically when vegetation is removed. This further reduces the potential of the ecosystem to recover.

In brief, these modifications — loss of nutrients, deterioration of air and soil microclimates, and soil erosion — bring about a complete change of the whole ecosystem. When such a change occurs in a 1- or 2-hectare plot, the system may recover. However, when the deforested area measures tens or hundreds of square kilometres, the process may be irreversible.

African forests

In Africa, forests are mainly removed for two reasons: they are cleared for new farmlands and they are cut for lumber and firewood. When old-growth forests are eliminated, productivity of the soil decreases because of nutrient losses. In most cases, the decrease in fertility is so great that even applying fertilizers does not result in competitive agricultural activity. For poor farmers, fertilizers are unaffordable, except in rare cases where natural fertilizers or phosphate rock are available locally. Often, the only practical way to increase production is to clear more forest area for cultivation.

In earlier times, shifting cultivation from one small plot to another allowed the ecosystem to recuperate. With increasing population density and encroachment of commercial plantations, however, recuperation has become impossible, and the forest ecosystem disappears completely, with the consequent loss of bio- and cultural diversity and water resources. Such pressures are causing African forests to retreat at a sustained rate.

In the 20th century, the main culprits have been commercial crops, such as bananas, oil palms, rubber, and cocoa. In Nigeria, oil palm plantations have replaced forests over large areas, particularly in the eastern regions of the country. Coupled with the rapid growth and concentration of the population,[6] this has left little forest remaining. In Côte d'Ivoire, about half a million hectares of forest are cleared annually to make room for cocoa, coffee, and other food products. From an area of 14 million hectares in 1956, the forest had been reduced to less than 5 million hectares 30 years later. The export of commercial crops and lumber explains the relative success of the country's economy in the short term; however, its unsustainability is evident.

---

[6] Nigeria's population is over 100 million in a territory of 800 thousand square kilometres.

Southeast Asian rain forests

In Southeast Asia, the originally extensive rain forests have been greatly reduced. In Burma, Indochina, and Thailand, forests have been replaced by farms and plantations. The forests of the more densely populated Indonesian islands (Java, Madura, Lombok, and Bali) have been logged or burned to the point where there are few remaining relics. As a result of deforestation on fragile soils, erosion has become a serious and widespread problem. In Java, annual erosion rates ranging from 10 to 40 tonnes per hectare have been reported. Recently, the drive toward deforestation has affected some areas that had remained untouched in Peninsular Malaysia, Sumatra, Mindanao (Philippines), and other less-populated islands of the region.

Large tracts of forest can still be found in Borneo (Kalimantan), New Guinea, and Celebes (Sulawesi). The Indonesian government attempted to promote settlement on these islands to alleviate the problems associated with the extremely high population density in Java (nearly 900 people per square kilometre). The initiative produced mixed results. To some degree, it relieved the population pressure in Java (although only temporarily). At the local level, however, the effect was disastrous. Large areas of rain forest were destroyed and the native people on the islands were displaced from their land. Javanese are alien to New Guinea and Borneo; the traditional cultures of these two large islands have been profoundly affected, and the process still continues.

The situation on Borneo is particularly complex. It belongs to three countries: unevenly populated Indonesia, a large multi-island country; oil-producing Brunei, which is small, rich, and densely populated; and the Malaysian states of Sarawak and Sabah. Deforestation and the annihilation of wildlife are still going on at a fast rate in the Indonesian part of Borneo, where settlement strategies have compiled a very poor record.

In Malaysia, until recently, authorities were not concerned with the preservation of the natural rain forests. In 1991, a Malaysian minister was quoted as saying: "It is not our business to supply the West with oxygen" (*Economist* 1993c). This attitude has changed somewhat. In October 1993, however, a major business deal was announced by a large company (owned by the Minister for Environment and Tourism) that involved a logging concession on 200 thousand hectares of rain forest, along with a coal mine and other components. Sarawak forests produce 80% of Malaysia's timber-related products, and Malaysian environmentalists predict that Borneo's rain forests will disappear in 20 years.

In other areas — for example, the Philippines, Thailand, and Sabah (on Borneo) — some tracts of rain forest are being conserved and the export of timber has been halted. Deforestation continues, but at a slower rate, mainly as a result of agricultural encroachment.

Until recently, the effects of deforestation were less pronounced in the eastern half of New Guinea (part of the republic of Papua New Guinea) and nearby islands (the Solomon Islands). In the last few years, however, the tropical hardwood timbers of these areas have been stripped beyond the level of sustainability. Francis Tilly, Prime Minister of the Solomon Islands, foresees the disappearance of all commercial timber from the islands in 15 years if this rate of deforestation continues. According to the *Economist* (1994a), landowners can get as little as $2.70 per cubic metre for their timber. The foreign buyer, however, can then sell this timber for as much as $350 per cubic metre! In the Solomon Islands and Papua New Guinea, most foreign logging companies are of Malaysian origin, escaping the increasingly tight controls on logging in their own country.

The Amazon rain forest

The quest for rubber, mainly after 1840, was one of the main factors in the settlement of the Amazon. In 1844, only 367 tonnes of rubber was exported from the region; in 1851, exports had increased to 1 391 tonnes and by 1910 to 42 000 tonnes. During this period, 600 to 700 thousand new settlers immigrated to the Amazon region as a direct or indirect result of the establishment of the plantations. The total population of the area, which was about 137 thousand in 1820, increased to 323 thousand in 1870 and to more than 1.2 million by 1910.

During this century, settlement of the Amazon has accelerated, mainly as a result of government policies promoting agriculture, cattle-raising, and logging in the region and bolstering a legal system that clearly favoured forest-clearing. A key element in this system was land allocation based on the concept of "squatter's rights"; title was awarded to whoever could demonstrate occupation of the land for a given period. Because occupation could be demonstrated by partial or total deforestation of the land to be claimed, systematic and widespread clearing of land for cultivation or speculation ensued.

Later, particularly after the discovery of the Serra Pelada gold deposits, mining activities developed, resulting in widespread degradation of the natural landscape and water resources. Gold was mined in open quarries, in mines, and in alluvial placers throughout the region, such as Mato Grosso and the Madeira River. Simultaneously, a number of other large-scale mining concerns, such as the iron and tin mines of Carajas, gradually spread throughout the region.

Another factor in the loss of forest habitat relates to the construction of large hydroelectric complexes, such as the Tucurui dam on the Tocantins River (with a flooded area of about 2 thousand square kilometres), the Samuel dam in Rondônia, and others.

Satellite images show that 410 thousand square kilometres of forest was cleared between 1978 and 1988 (Salati 1991). This amounts to almost 10% of the whole area, reducing total forest cover to slightly more than 4.5 million square kilometres. Of the approximately 425 thousand square kilometres of the Amazon that was cleared by the early 1990s, about three-quarters was eliminated in the last two decades (Preston 1991). At the same time, the Colombian Amazon forest (with a total area of about 280 thousand square kilometres) had been reduced by 7% to 260 thousand square kilometres, and the forests of the Peruvian Amazon had shrunk by about 60 thousand square kilometres (Salati 1991). Recent news from the Amazon region reveals a slowing of the deforestation process. In 1990, "only" 14 thousand square kilometres was cleared, compared with almost 20 thousand in 1989 and about 27 thousand square kilometres in 1988 (Preston 1991).

In Ecuador, the main problems resulted from petroleum exploitation. Frequent spills in the Ecuadorean oil fields have had a critical effect on the environment. One of the largest spills took place in the region of La Joya de los Sachas, affecting the Napo River basin (Varea

1992). Similar spills are frequent in Colombia, where the main oil pipelines are frequently attacked by guerrilla forces.

Significant effects of deforestation have been described by Salati and Nobre (1991) based on an empirical model developed by Shuttleworth (1988). From September 1983 to September 1985, about 10% of the rainfall in the study area of Salati and Nobre was intercepted by the forest canopy, accounting for 20 to 25% of the evaporation. The remainder of the water being returned to the air moved through the trees by transpiration. Over the same period, about half of the incoming precipitation returned to the atmosphere as evaporation, a process requiring 90% of the energy input. Of net radiation, 75% went into evaporating water and the remaining 25% was used to heat the air (Salati and Nobre 1991). It is estimated that 50 to 60% of the rainfall in the region originates from the recirculated water vapour that arises through evapotranspiration. Thus, a reduction in the forest cover will decrease precipitation, perhaps up to one-half or more throughout the Amazon and in downwind regions, such as the Bolivian altiplano and the eastern slopes of the Andes.

Palaeogeographic studies show that less-humid periods were relatively common during the Quaternary period in the Amazon region. Colinvaux (1989) thinks that these changes were one of the causes of the high level of biodiversity in the area and that they coincided approximately with the glacial period:

> The contemporary reality is that much of the Amazon basin will be turned into pasture as people clear the land for cattle grazing.... History does suggest that parts of the Amazon can be exploited productively without causing mass extinction, but wise use must be the overriding theme.

Despite the modifications that the area suffered in previous eras, for the last few thousand years the core of the great forest has remained largely unchanged despite demonstrated human occupation. The production systems developed during that time did not bring about the general degradation that is occurring now in newly settled areas. It is generally accepted that indigenous production systems are sustainable over the long term. Although we are not certain what the forest was like before human occupation, we do know that the current forest ecosystem is the result of indigenous management for several millennia. That management system was based on a careful slash-and-burn technique, where small patches of forest were cleared for planting, used for 3 or 4 years, and then abandoned, allowing the selective growth of new plants. Other areas were preserved as sources of medicinal plants, for example, or simply left alone. Under these management strategies, some areas of the forest were used without affecting their potential, and the rest of the ecosystem was protected, resulting in long-term conservation of local environments. In that way, people took advantage of the enormous diversity of the jungle; rather than attempting to obtain maximum immediate return, they ensured the optimum long-term benefits.

Temperate forests

Despite a long history of deforestation, temperate forests still occupy a vast area: 1 933 million hectares, compared with the 1 700 million hectares of tropical forests that remains today. More than 80% of the world's remaining temperate forest is found in North America and Eurasia (Table 2).

Most temperate forests are managed using interventionist strategies. Some are managed reasonably well, maintaining many components of the original ecosystems. In others, the indigenous ecosystem has been

Table 2. Worldwide distribution of temperate forests.

Region	Area (million hectares)	Proportion of total (%)
Former USSR	944	48.8
North America	620	32.1
Europe	157	8.1
Temperate Asia	94	4.9
Temperate South America	68	3.5
Oceania	40	2.1
Africa	10	0.5
Total	1 933	100.0

Source: FAO (1988, pp. 47–58).

completely replaced with "artificial" (often exotic) plantations. Exploitation of temperate forests for lumber and other resources has led not only to a decrease in forested areas but also to a loss of biodiversity. In many cases, inappropriate management has produced negative effects on the living systems and on the supporting environment, such as substantial changes in the structure of the forest, a decrease in the number of species, and damage to wild fauna. In tree plantations, the negative effects are even greater because these "artificial ecosystems" are normally monospecific.

In southern Chile, for example, the indigenous temperate forests were rich and diverse. Traditionally, they were used by the Mapuche and other local populations. Today, however, they are being supplanted by exotic monospecific plantations of trees grown for export (such as *Pinus insigne*). The negative environmental effects and the loss of diversity (both biological and cultural) that this practice is producing are becoming widely recognized.

Although temperate forests still cover large areas, their actual value has been reduced because of diminished diversity and other ecological changes. The continued use of forests in cool climates has recently become less economic because of their slow growth and increasing opposition from environmentalist groups (particularly in North America).

Soybeans and deforestation

Health-conscious people of the developed countries have discovered a food staple that is the "remedy to all ills" — soybeans. Rich in protein and low in cholesterol, they have become the diet supplement of the 1990s for those who want to decrease their risk of cancer and heart disease. The soybean plant is native to east Asia. It was domesticated by the Chinese about 4 thousand years ago and has become a component of the diet of people in most east Asian countries. Per-capita consumption has traditionally been high in China, Indonesia, Japan, Korea, Myanmar, and Thailand, probably one of the reasons for the low rates of heart disease and cancer in this region.

Western countries have known about and consumed soybeans since the time of Marco Polo, but only recently has this staple become important in the diet of their populations. In the 1980s, the increase in soybean use was particularly dramatic as a result of its growing popularity as an animal feed. In the United States, soybean use doubled, and similar trends were observed in Canada and several countries of the European Community (in the Netherlands, for example, soybeans are widely used as pig feed).

World production has followed the trend, growing substantially in the last few years. In the United States, production of soybeans increased from 1.1 to 1.9 million bushels between 1970 and 1987. Some increase in production also occurred in Europe and Asia; however, most of the increased demand has been met by clearing forestland for soybean production in South America. Argentina and Brazil are the largest producers of soybeans on the continent; Bolivia and Paraguay have also substantially increased production recently. Other South American countries are important suppliers, but produce smaller volumes.

The crop — For higher productivity, soybeans require well-drained, highly fertile soils; high temperatures; and abundant rainfall. The most appropriate soils for soybean production are sandy and silty tropical soils in humid areas that are not subject to regular flooding. The best results are obtained if soybeans are planted immediately after deforestation. For this reason, soybean producers have identified the large forest regions of South America as the best places for their farms.

Normally, trees are cut and sold and the stumps removed using heavy machinery. After other vegetation is cleared away, plots are prepared for soybean cultivation. Often, soybeans are planted in combination with other crops on a semiannual rotation. The crop normally associated with soybeans is wheat. The additional demand on the soil resulting from multicropping increases the rate at which some key nutrients (potassium and phosphorus) are depleted, although, because soybean is a leguminous vegetable, it replenishes nitrogen in the soil.

Tropical soils can sustain soybeans and associated crops for 3 or 4 years before their fertility is affected. Once the level of key nutrients decreases, productivity and yields also decrease and fertilizers must be applied. Because using fertilizer increases costs and reduces competitiveness and earnings, soybean farming companies and entrepreneurs often prefer to clear new, inexpensive forestland. This practice has resulted in systematic clearing of the tropical rain forest throughout the Mato Grosso–Santa Cruz–Paraguay region.

Tropical soybean production areas extend throughout central and southeastern Brazil, eastern Bolivia, and Paraguay, in addition to temperate regions in Argentina, Uruguay, and the Brazilian state of Rio Grande do Sul. As of the mid-1990s, soybeans are the most important item in the commercial agricultural economy of South America.

Effects on forest soils — Soybean farming in tropical soils causes much damage. Forest cover is eliminated, the soil remains bare or poorly protected for most of the year, erosion becomes widespread, rills and gullies develop, and gradually soil fertility is lost along with much of the soil itself. For this reason, the continued use of tropical soils requires heavy applications of fertilizer; when this is not possible, the land is used to raise cattle or is abandoned.

Soybean crops are affected by a large number of plagues. Among the insects that attack the plant are *Auticassia gemmatalis*, *Rachiplusia mu*, *Pseudoplisia includens*, *Nezara viridula*, *Peizodums guildinii*, *Euschistus heros*, and others at a more local level. In addition, soybeans are attacked by numerous nematodes, fungi, bacteria, and viruses. The crops are also frequently invaded by several local and exotic weeds, reducing productivity levels (Souza dos Santos 1988). To keep the crops healthy, farmers apply large volumes of agrochemicals to combat weeds, insects, and other pests. Some of these chemicals find their way into natural water systems, causing serious contamination not only in local streams but in swamplands as well.

As a result, soybean cultivation is degrading local ecosystems, and its expansion can only be explained by a lack of concern at political and local levels about the long-term integrity of these systems. The growth of soybean cultivation in South America has continued unabated for some time. Since the late 1970s, it has been the main crop in the upper

Paraguay basin. In 1985, total production in Mato Grosso was 1.7 million tonnes and in Mato Grosso do Sul, 2.6 million tonnes. This represented over 20% of total Brazilian production or almost 5% of world production. If Bolivian and Paraguayan production are included, the total volume for the basin was about 6 million tonnes in 1985 (7% of world production).

During the last decade, expansion continued. In 1993–1994, annual production was 4.8 million tonnes for Mato Grosso (almost three times what it was 9 years earlier) and 2.3 million tonnes in Mato Grosso do Sul. Almost 10% of the current world supply of soybeans comes from the upper Paraguay basin, where the total area planted is about 3.5 million hectares and crop yields are about 2 tonnes per hectare.

Effects on rivers — The radical change in vegetation cover over such a vast region is influencing the hydrologic regime in rivers downstream. The principal rivers affected are the upper tributaries of the Paraguay (the Taquari and Cuaiabá rivers) and Paraná (the Iguazú, Grande, Paranapanema, and Tietê rivers) and, to a lesser extent, some Amazon tributaries flowing from the south (such as the Xingu and Tapajoz rivers).

The main effects of deforestation have been increased runoff, higher flood peaks, soil erosion, larger amounts of suspended sediments in the water, rapid silting of dams, longer droughts, and generally more irregular flows in rivers throughout the year. However, a hydrologic feature of the region tends to even out these irregular flows — the Gran Pantanal wetland.

Gran Pantanal

Gran Pantanal (Figure 1) is a large region of swamps and marshland in southwestern Mato Grosso, Brazil. Extending for about 160 kilometres along the east bank of the upper Paraguay River, it resembles an interior delta formed as a result of Quaternary and pre-Quaternary sedimentation in a slowly sinking basin located to the west of the Gondwanic

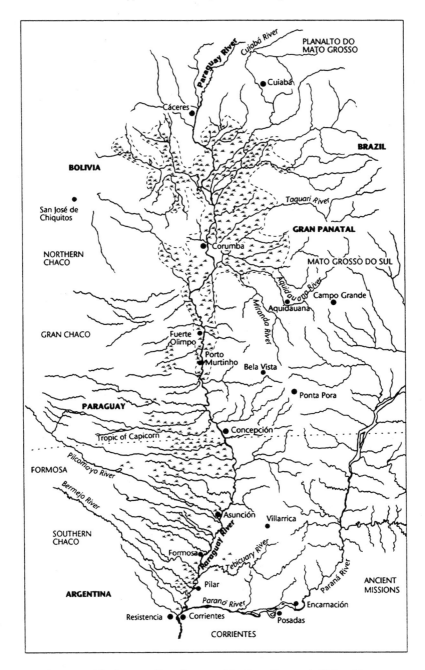

Figure 1. The Paraguay River basin and the Gran Pantanal of Mato Grosso.

basalts and sandstones of Mesozoic and Cenozoic age (such as the Botucatu sandstones) and the Brazilian Shield.

Rivers descending from the north and east arrive at the plain and produce enormous alluvial fans that obstruct the development of river valleys. This causes the formation of a characteristic meandering pattern as the riverbeds frequently change direction, leaving abandoned crescent-shaped lakes. The landscape is dotted with hundreds of lakes where aquatic organisms, waterfowl, and many other species flourish. Several well-defined rivers can also be identified, such as the Paraguay (the main river) and the Cuiabá, Taquari, Miranda, and Aquidabuana.

Before occupation by Europeans and criollos, the region mainly consisted of humid forest in the lowlands and *cerrado* in the neighbouring highlands. The ecosystems are intermediate between the Atlantic forest and the Amazon rain forest. *Cerrado* (the Spanish word for closed) is also a type of forest with a lower canopy and a bushier, grassier undergrowth. There is no sharp boundary between the *cerrado* and the humid forest; a gradual transition can be observed almost everywhere.

The level of biodiversity in the region was (and to a large extent still is) high; it includes tens of thousands of plant species, hundreds of thousands of invertebrates, and many fish, birds, and mammals. As a result of this natural richness, the area was densely populated during precolonial times. Conservative estimates put the population of the Gran Pantanal basin at no fewer than 1 million.

The arrival of the Europeans was traumatic. Spaniards came from the west (upper areas of Peru) and the south (Asunción) and established religious missions in the Guairá region about 500 kilometres southeast of the Pantanal. Paulist slave traders (the *Bandeirantes*) reached the Guairá region by the end of the 17th century. They captured tens of thousands of indigenous people in the missions and villages and sold them to the owners of the sugarcane plantations of Pernambuco.

Despite the conquest and colonization efforts, however, both the regional ecosystem and portions of the local populations managed to survive until well into the 20th century. Most of the Pantanal remained in the Empire and later Republic of Brazil, some lies in Bolivia, and

Paraguay retained only the small area of wetlands in the Gran Chaco and Ñeembucú.

During the first half of the 20th century, activity centred around the Paraguay River, as *quebracho* wood was harvested for tannin and *yerba mate* plantations were established. In the 1960s and 1970s, criollo occupation increased following new Brazilian "development" policies that made new highways and roads a priority and encouraged uncontrolled colonization. Tens of thousands of migrants (from Rio Grande do Sul and other areas of Brazil) moved to Mato Grosso, establishing ranches throughout the region.

One common "style" of occupation was to clear the *cerrado* and forest, plant grasses, and introduce cattle. Deforestation was also carried out to prepare land for planting grains, mainly soybeans, rice, and corn. Rice plantations were established everywhere, mainly to obtain funding from the government. According to local agronomists, the rice plantations were a means to obtain easy credits. The forest was logged and removed or burned to make room for dry rice farming. After 3 or 4 years, grass seeds were included in the rice and, after 4 to 6 years, a new artificial grassy ecosystem was established.

On more fertile soils, the forest was cleared for soybean farming. In the early 1990s, soybean agriculture occupied 5 to 10% of the land in the Pantanal basin, and soybeans are the main agricultural export of the Brazilian states of Mato Grosso and Mato Grosso do Sul. Soybean production is also important in Santa Cruz (Bolivia) and eastern Paraguay.

Deforestation took place quickly; by the early 1990s, extensive areas had been cleared. In Mato Grosso do Sul, for example, 80% of the forest is gone. In the Gran Pantanal, deforestation was delayed somewhat because of the swampy conditions. Gradually, however, local ranchers have encroached on the natural ecosystem by burning trees or using "agrotoxic" substances. Many thousands of hectares of forest and swamp have been destroyed to make room for raising cattle.

The effects of this environmental degradation are being felt throughout the Pantanal region. The ancient, clear rivers have become brownish, muddy streams. Channels are being filled by sand, fishing is uncontrolled, and poaching of local animals is widespread (often organized by the ranchers themselves). The few remaining indigenous people have been dispossessed of their land and reduced to a situation of misery and desperation.

Impact of changes in the Gran Pantanal

The Pantanal is a huge natural-flow regulator. The plain covers 90 thousand square kilometres and receives water from rivers on the west, north, and east during the rainy season. Some of the water is lost to evaporation; the rest moves toward the southern outlet to form a free-flowing river (the Paraguay) several hundred kilometres to the south. The summer rainy season occurs in January and February, but the surplus flow of water in the Paraguay River is spread over the next 6 months because of the presence of the Pantanal.

Because of the Gran Pantanal, the peak flow period for the Alto Paraná and the Paraguay rivers occurs at different times of the year: the Alto Paraná reaches its maximum level in March and the Paraguay a few months later between June and August. Without the dampening effect of the Pantanal, flooding would occur at the same time in these rivers, causing disastrous flooding downstream of their confluence. During the rest of the year, river levels would be much lower, affecting navigation and the movement of merchandise to and from Rosario, Santa Fe, Paraná, and all of Paraguay.

The sediment-loaded waters of the Bermejo and Pilcomayo rivers also affect the level of the Paraguay. These rivers arise in the highlands of Salta, Jujuy, and the Bolivian altiplano. Their peak flow period occurs in late summer or early fall. Without the Pantanal, this peak would coincide with a period of heavy flow in the Paraguay, with potentially catastrophic consequences up- and downstream from their confluence.

In brief, widespread deforestation in the Paraguay River basin combined with drainage of the Pantanal wetlands would significantly increase the flow in this river in summer and early fall. It would result in a much larger sediment load throughout the basin, and flood peaks in the river and its tributaries would be simultaneous. The volume that could be expected has not been calculated, but it would probably be at

1.
The Hidrovia project

In the midst of ever-increasing damage to local ecosystems, a new regional integration project — Hidrovia — has been proposed. The aim of the project is to ensure that soybeans and beef, among other products, can be transported from the river ports of Mato Grosso and Bolivia (in Gran Pantanal and upstream) down to Buenos Aires in Argentina and Nueva Palmira in Uruguay for export. Today, the Pantanal can be navigated only by small boats and barges. Its river channels are already shallow and are filling with silt and sand. In fact, this situation created the swamp in the first place.

For commercial navigation to be feasible, deeper canals and complementary hydroworks may have to be built. Digging canals in the swamp, however, will have an impact on both the geo- and ecosystem. An immediate effect will be an increase in water velocity in the channels and erosion of the banks and riverbed. This process will occur first downstream, moving gradually upstream and resulting in widespread drainage of the swamp. The drier soils will then be available for use as rangeland. The aquatic ecosystem will be disturbed by noise, turbulence, and contamination from the expected heavy barge traffic.

The project may require the movement of millions of tonnes of earth and sediment and the use of heavy equipment and numerous labourers. One can only guess at the destructive effects of this work on wildlife and the ecological equilibrium. However, an independent investigation must be carried out to ensure that all factors are taken into account before a decision about the project can be made. This need is widely recognized by university researchers, local nongovernmental organizations (NGOs), and some political groups and authorities.

least twice the current highest flow in the Paraguay River and slightly less than twice the highest flow in the middle Paraná.

Winter and spring flows, on the other hand, would be greatly reduced (probably several times lower throughout the basin), affecting navigation and the water supply of certain cities — this is already occurring in Cuiabá, Mato Grosso.

Several waterworks have been built in the Paraná basin. The most important was the Itaipu dam, downstream of the largest falls (in terms of flow volume) in the world — Sete Quedas Falls. This dam, which cost over $10 billion, was completed around 1982, forming a 2 thousand square kilometre lake and producing a significant quantity of hydroelectric power. Although the energy produced is to be shared equally by

Brazil and Paraguay, Paraguay uses only 5% of its share. The remaining 95% is sometimes purchased by Brazil or, lately, not used at all. Selling this energy to other countries is not permitted under the binational treaty.

Despite the huge amount of unused energy generated by the Itaipu dam, the governments of Argentina and Paraguay decided to construct a new mega-dam at Yacyreta Island (about 300 kilometres downstream of Itaipu). The cost of this dam may be over $5 billion and it will contribute a significant amount of energy to the already enormous surpluses existing in the region.

More recently, plans are under way to create a "hidrovia" or "hydro-way" to ensure river navigability through a complex array of dams, drainage and navigation canals, docks, piers, and other harbour structures (see box 1). The cost of the project might reach several billion dollars, adding to the considerable foreign debt of the countries along the Paraguay and Paraná rivers. There is concern that these works may result in the virtual elimination of the Pantanal and that they will be useless, as canals remain dry for most of the year and flood catastrophically during peak flow periods.

The final result of these mega-plans may not be "development" or even "modernization," but the complete annihilation of some of the world's largest ecosystems, together with their associated traditional cultures. Some foresee a significant loss of opportunities, natural and human resources, and future financing possibilities for the countries and cities of the basin.

Indigenous people of the upper Paraguay basin

Despite aggressive occupation of their lands, attempts to eliminate or enslave them, migration, and acculturation, about 60 thousand indigenous people belonging to 15 nations have managed to survive in the Pantanal–upper Paraguay region. These people were evicted from their land in most of the *cerrado* regions of Mato Grosso, remaining only in isolated areas with less-fertile, stony soils or on steep hillsides and in the swamplands of Gran Pantanal. Several groups are in danger of extinction.

2.
The Guarani were right

Before "science," humans knew many things. Traditional knowledge was not supported by a theoretical framework, but it was rich and diverse. Tribes understood their environment: vegetation, insects, mammals, birds. They knew which plants could be used as medicines and which were poisonous. Knowledge was site-specific. In most cases, it was difficult to apply elsewhere; but locally, it allowed many groups to sustain a quality of life that should not be undervalued.

Scientific knowledge accumulated slowly. In many ways, it was nourished by the traditional or "empirical" knowledge of local groups. After many generations, scientists are still looking to traditional societies for elements of knowledge.

Some scientists, however, possessing the knowledge accumulated over generations, prefer to ignore the fact that traditional knowledge, in one way or another, provides the basic insights that allow continuing enrichment of the paths of science and technology. In the meantime, a huge body of knowledge about nature and its ways is being lost with the death of each shaman, wise man, and medicine woman.

Agronomists have failed in their attempt to increase production indefinitely with their "green revolution." Twenty years later, whole ecosystems have disappeared, taking with them species that were not even recorded. Hundreds of crop varieties have been wiped from the face of the Earth and erosion has become widespread. Although more food was produced for a period of time, our children and our children's children will not be able to grow crops in eroded soils. Monospecific, artificial ecosystems are vulnerable to plagues and require large quantities of pesticides that are contaminating water resources.

Dead fish, eroded soils, unique animals and plants eliminated — the technologists have failed. The Guarani knew how to clear a parcel of land; what, when, where, and how to plant; how to leave large areas untouched to conserve the medicines and to keep the spirits happy. The Guarani called them "spirits"; scientists call it "genetic biodiversity." Basically, it is the same thing. The Guarani were right.

The Guarani people of Mato Grosso do Sul number about 30 thousand; they live on about 20 reserves, but the population is concentrated in small areas. During colonization, their religious leaders were ignored by the government and *capitaos* were appointed to govern them. The Guaranis resisted this move by continuing their rituals in secret and, later, by reviving some of their traditional systems of self-government (like communal assembly). The difficult situation in Guarani communities is reflected in the rate of suicides among the young people (31 cases in 1990, 21 in 1991, and 21 in 1992), which is among the highest in the world (see box 2).

The Guato people build canoes. They live by fishing and farming the islands of the Paraguay River. Only a few hundred Guatos still exist and only a few of these remember their own language.

The Guaycuru-Kadiweu belong to an ancient, large, seminomadic nation that became horseback riders in the 17th century. They lost some of their land in Mato Grosso in the 1950s and were left with a reserve of just over 500 thousand hectares. There are currently fewer than 1 500 Kadiweus living on their ancestral lands and a few hundred living elsewhere.

The Terena, who are descendants of the Arawak, are among the largest groups of indigenous people, numbering about 20 thousand. They farm (rice, beans, manioc, and corn) and display a high level of acculturation. Like other indigenous groups, they have had difficulty retaining enough land for survival. Today, they are virtually landless and depend largely on low-paying jobs on local ranches.

As in many other areas of the continent, the situation of the indigenous people of Mato Grosso is critical and, in many cases, desperate. A wealth of traditional knowledge is being lost every day, human rights are violated, and many indigenous people who are unable to visualize a future for themselves take their own lives. Along with nature's riches, Mato Grosso is losing its rich ethnic and cultural diversity and the knowledge necessary to ensure a more sustainable and just future.

5

Grasslands

Savannas

Savannas are extensive tropical grassland areas that cover more than 10 million square kilometres of the Earth. The largest expanses are found in Africa (nearly 4 million square kilometres), South America, and, to a lesser degree, Asia and Australia. The dominant vegetation in savannas is usually grasses, intercalated with shrubs and trees. In some cases, shrubs and trees dominate, and savannas evolve into other ecosystems, such as:

- *cerrado* — a type of forest with a lower canopy and a bushier, grassier undergrowth (see Chapter 4);

- *caatinga* — a low-density, xerophytic ecosystem of bushes and shrubs with some trees characteristic of northeastern Brazil;

- *chaco* — a more xerophytic forest of low trees and bushes in extensive flatlands of Paraguay and northern Argentina; or

- *sudan* — herbaceous ecosystems with intercalated trees extending from the valley of the Nile to the Atlantic Ocean along the low tropical latitudes north of the equator.

The main characteristic of present-day savannas is their periodic (usually annual) water deficit. Both vegetation and fauna have adapted to it. Plants, for example, have developed deciduous aerial systems (leaves) and an annual cycle of growth.

Not all savannas are primary ecosystems (which evolve with little or no human intervention). Many, perhaps most, are secondary ecosystems (which result from human action). Frequently, shrubby, bushy, or forest areas have been and are being burned to make way for agriculture, raising cattle, or hunting. It is difficult to know to what extent today's savannas are the result of a transformation of other preexisting ecosystems rather than naturally occurring. In Africa, the "savannization" process started very early. Setting forest fires is a common hunting strategy in many societies and Africa was the home of hunters for several hundred thousand years (if not millions).

It is likely that fragile, nongrassy ecosystems gave rise to savanna or even steppe environments perhaps as early as the mid-Pleistocene. Obviously, climate also changed during this geological epoch. During humid periods, savannization of deserts and encroachment of forests into savannas took place. However, the effects of geological changes during the last few hundred thousand years have been somewhat obscured by the impacts of continued human action.

After domestication of herbivorous animals and the spread of agriculture (starting about 10 thousand years ago, but intensifying during the last 3 thousand years), the processes of environmental savannization progressed further. Savannization of the Sudanese region is probably related to domestication of sorghum and millet and to the adaptation of previously domesticated animals to local environments — mainly cattle, goats, and sheep, but later also dromedaries in the Sahelian periphery. In the late 19th century and first half of the 20th century, after widespread European colonization, new commercial crops were introduced (such as peanuts), population growth accelerated, and new forested areas were cleared, transforming most of intertropical Africa into savannas. The remaining forests are retreating at a rapid rate.

In South America, the process of savannization is recent. When the Europeans arrived in the 16th century, there were few, if any,

Ancient rock carvings in Hanakiyah, Arabian Desert, depict what are probably the first domesticated cattle (10 thousand years ago).

typical savannas. Most South American intertropical ecosystems are in subhumid climates with seasonal rains. Apparently during the humid subperiod of the mid-Quaternary, these areas were covered by trees or bushy vegetation (*cerrado* and *chaco*). In more arid areas, a less-dense, shrubby or bushy steppe vegetation developed (*caatinga*). Grasslands were restricted to temperate areas, particularly in the southern cone — the pampas and to the northern llanos.

The temperate grasslands

The temperate grasslands were planted with crops such as wheat and barley very early in history. Farming was widespread on all primary prairies of the Eurasian continent, especially in the Ukraine and southern Russia. Similar activities took place later in other regions of the world: the South American pampas, the North American prairies, the South African rangelands, and southeastern Australia. The remaining grasslands are often secondary (regrowth after cessation of agriculture); they are associated with intensive cattle-farming activities (such as dairy farming); or their soils are inappropriate for farming (too stony, rocky, or sandy, or grassy wetland).

In some countries, grasslands with agricultural potential can remain relatively unaffected for various reasons, such as inadequate access to markets or cultural history. This situation exists in South America and, to a lesser degree, in Australia, Texas, and the Transvaal of South Africa.

A typical surviving prairie ecosystem is found in the South American pampas. The pampas are flat or undulating landscapes extending for about a million square kilometres between 28° and 40°S latitude and east of the 500-millimetre isohyet. This isohyet (a line on a map joining points of similar precipitation) is the approximate boundary between the semi-arid and subhumid areas of temperate South America.

The Buenos Aires pampas are flat and largely used for farming, particularly in the more humid zones (with more than 750 millimetres of rainfall per year). East of the Paraná River, the flatlands gradually become more undulating and, in Uruguay and Rio Grande do Sul, Brazil, undulating and flat areas are interspersed with hilly landscapes. It is in these areas that grasslands have remained less disturbed by farming.

It is important to note that the South American pampas are grasslands not because trees cannot grow, but because they cannot compete with the grasses. Human intervention can radically change this situation through the deliberate planting of trees, which are typically exotic but occasionally indigenous. However, artificial forests in the pampas remained a limited phenomenon until very recently.

Modifying grassland ecosystems

Globalization of the economy and encroachment of land-intensive and labour-intensive agriculture on some savanna lands is producing some important environmental changes. Undulating and hilly savannas are being eroded by water, reducing the thickness of their soils and, consequently, their agricultural potential. In flatter areas, soils are less affected by water, but may be seriously degraded by aeolian (wind) action. Irrigation may also have long-term consequences, such as water-logging, salinization, or alkalinization.

In all cases, repeated cultivation of the same plots brings about a gradual loss of nutrients, reducing fertility and having a negative effect on the biological potential of the exploited areas. When fertilizers are used to compensate for decreasing fertility, other side effects can occur. Not all soil nutrients are replaced by the application of fertilizers; some, especially micronutrients, may not be added, and some impoverishment takes place in any case. Second, some nutrients may be applied in excessive volumes with potential deleterious effects, not only on the soil, but also on the natural water systems, giving rise to algal growth and, in some cases, to eutrophication of lakes and reservoirs.

Pesticides can have an even greater impact because of their natural toxicity (obviously, the main purpose of pesticides is to kill pests). They may find their way not only into the leaves, fruit, and vegetative tissues of crops, but also into surface water bodies and groundwater. Some long-lasting pesticides may appear a few years after their application in the water supply of nearby towns or rural communities.

One of the land uses of savannas, particularly in Africa, is for raising livestock. In drier savannas or in steppes, overgrazing can produce extensive desertification patterns. This can be seen in many African countries (particularly in the Sahelian region), where overgrazing has reduced vegetation density and diversity, promoting soil erosion, decay, and loss of productivity.

An important factor associated with overgrazing is the indiscriminate drilling of wells in the countryside. In pastoral societies, cattle ownership is frequently a sign of prestige. Raising animals can be an important social function, allowing a man to find a wife or to obtain more power. The main factor limiting the size of a herd has always been the availability of water. Areas around the main water holes are heavily overgrazed, but peripheral areas may be almost intact. When many new wells are drilled, people increase their herds and move them into the new locations. After a few years, the whole landscape is degraded beyond recognition and irreversible desertification takes place. Examples of this situation can be found throughout the African continent — northern Senegal (Kerkhof 1992, pp. 105–112), northern Kenya, Sudan, Mali, and Niger.

In South America, a number of savanna ecosystems are being used for agricultural purposes. Those of Brazil are typical. The savanna areas of southern and central Brazil have developed as a result of the removal of forests. In Mato Grosso, the tropical rain forest, which was slightly less dense than the Amazon jungle, was gradually burned and logged to make way for various crops, particularly rice and soybeans.

In dry rice farming, fertilizers are usually not applied. Thus, the nutrients in the soil, which, like most tropical soils, has low fertility, are further reduced and the land quickly becomes inappropriate for further cultivation — without heavy applications of costly fertilizers. Normally, after 3 or 4 years of dry rice cultivation, the land is no longer productive and is converted to cattle ranching. (The secondary savanna in Mato Grosso is a low-productivity rangeland for cattle.)

Soybean cultivation is carried out on a large scale, for commercial purposes, on large farms using a similar nonsustainable approach. Fertilizers and pesticides are applied with little concern for the environment, seriously affecting the aquatic ecosystems in nearby streams. Many indigenous communities of South America that depend on fish for their existence have seen their livelihood and incomes curtailed because of aggressive agricultural practices in these secondary savanna lands (see also Chapter 4).

In southern Brazil, from São Paulo to Rio de Janeiro, the original vegetation was subtropical rain forest and an almost monospecific ecosystem of *Araucaria* (Brazilian pine). São Paulo's forest was gradually eliminated, at the end of the 19th century and during the first half of the 20th century, to make way for coffee plantations and other crops. In many places, a savanna-type vegetation has replaced the forest. More recently, sugarcane (for alcohol fuel production) has been planted throughout the São Paulo region, often supplanting coffee plantations. The *Araucaria* forest suffered a similar fate. From the 1950s through the 1970s, almost all of the forest was logged; ranching and cultivation of crops such as soybean now occur on the secondary savannas that

Zebu cattle is widely used in Brazilian rangelands.

developed. In some cases, the *Araucaria* forests were replaced with artificial forests of exotic trees.

Modification of natural ecosystems may have unexpected effects on neighbouring farming systems. Planting some types of trees can alter the nesting habits of some birds and favour their reproduction. For example, if a bird's natural predators cannot reach the nest, the species may reproduce without constraint. Many crops, including sunflowers, corn, and fruit trees, can be severely affected by increases in the number of budgies and pigeons. Some of these birds may have wide ranges (more than 50 kilometres) and, therefore, may affect crops some distance from their nesting area. Exotic trees (such as pine trees in South American prairies) may also provide a feeding area for birds or insects. Indiscriminate planting of such trees in grasslands and associated farming areas can have a significant destabilizing effect on both the natural ecosystems and the crops.

The eucalyptus tree, which is native to Australia, has a very high growth rate. Because of this, they are planted throughout the world for many purposes. Eucalyptus is also a good nesting tree. It grows to 30 metres or more and, therefore, is difficult for grassland predators (mammals and other vertebrates) to climb. Frequently, farmland close

3.

Planting trees in grassland ecosystems

Lately, as a result of globalization and the transfer of labour- and land-intensive activities to developing countries, large-scale forestation has reached the pampas. The trees used are mainly eucalyptus and pine: *Eucalyptus globulus, E. grandis, E. rostrata, Pinus pinaster,* and *P. maritimus.* Large tracts of former grasslands have been dedicated to monospecific plantations of these trees, which are grown for lumber, fuel, or paper pulp, often for export, but also for consumption in the pampas countries.

The consequences of this widespread planting of exotic trees are becoming apparent. Indigenous trees are not very tall and are sparsely distributed. The new, exotic trees offer an interesting nesting niche for many birds that have spread beyond their natural habitat.

The prairie predators of birds — raccoons, foxes, opossums, wildcats — are unable to climb the tall trees, resulting in an population explosion of some species of birds, such as budgies and wild pigeons. These birds plague nearby crops, reducing their quality or destroying them completely.

Although the eucalyptus plantations are the main nesting habitat, they do not provide a feeding ground for birds; there is little or no undergrowth in the forests and the seeds of eucalyptus trees cannot be eaten by most birds. As a result, birds make feeding forays into nearby agricultural crops. These crops supply food for only a few months of the year, usually late spring to fall. Artificial pine plantations provide food for the birds during winter. The frequent association of eucalyptus and pine trees in agricultural areas can be a recipe for disaster. Eucalyptus trees provide a nesting place, pine trees the winter food, and crops the main staple for the rest of the year. A new artificial ecosystem is formed, but it is not in the best interests of farmers nor does it contribute to local biodiversity (Gutierrez et al. 1993).

to eucalyptus forests is plagued by an overabundance of birds that nest on the upper branches of the eucalyptus trees, where they thrive in the absence of predators that otherwise could prevent their multiplication (see box 3).

In addition, eucalyptus has been pinpointed as a strong "aridifier." Poore and Fries (1987) found that, by its third year, *Eucalyptus grandis* reduced stream flow (measured as equivalent millimetres of rainfall) by between 300 and 380 millimetres per year. In Nigeria, Sharda et al. (1988) found that eucalyptus trees reduced the amount of water flowing from a basin by about 23%. Similar studies in India revealed a decrease in runoff of 28% (Poore and Fries 1987).

Eucalyptus also effects soil fertility. A decrease in soil nutrients, such as phosphorus, has been recorded in many cases. However, the main effects on fertility come from logging, which removes large volumes of key elements from the ecosystem, reducing its potential for other uses. After eucalyptus trees have been harvested two to four times — over about 30 years — the land is rendered useless for any other productive purpose. Not only do the soils become infertile and dry, but they are also crisscrossed by the remains of many root systems. Farming is impossible without major, expensive corrective measures, which are not cost-effective for most agricultural activities. For all practical purposes, "eucalyptus soils" are no longer usable for farming.

In a number of African projects, described in *Agroforestry in Africa* (Kerkhof 1992), eucalyptus trees were introduced to traditional African societies without much consideration of their suitability to local ecosystems or cultures. As in Uruguay, the effects have frequently been deleterious to the local environment or quality of life. In spite of this result, strong pressure and funding is coming from many sources to expand this nonsustainable type of forestation. Uruguay, for example, received over $50 million from international banks for such forestation projects.

Environmental balance in grassland ecosystems

The balance of the effects (actual and potential) of globalization in the grasslands is unfavourable. Most savannas are the result of the degradation of forests. Although their soils are fertile, the fertility is often inherited from the former ecosystem and is substantially lower than it would be for a climatic savanna. Continuous farming on savannas gradually reduces fertility and, unless fertilizers are applied, agriculture becomes unproductive. In many cases, the use of fertilizers makes farming uneconomical and savanna lands are abandoned for other uses, usually raising cattle or planting with exotic trees, further unbalancing the ecosystem. Where slopes are steeper, the soft, highly friable savanna soils are easily eroded, further reducing their productivity.

These ecological changes bring about important geomorphologic and hydrologic changes. Gullies and ravines are formed by erosion, and stream-flow patterns become irregular (more severe droughts, increased frequency and intensity of floods). Navigation canals may be blocked by sediments, dams and reservoirs may become useless (or their life span may be considerably reduced), water intakes may became clogged, water-treatment plants become more difficult and costly to operate, and so on.

Environmental degradation of prairies is also frequently the result of increased runoff, soil erosion, and related geodynamic phenomena. In addition, there is a growing risk of soil deterioration as a result of careless forestation.

The belief that "planting trees is good" does not necessarily hold in grassland areas, where forestation may bring about an ecological imbalance that may end in a substantial reduction not only in productivity, but also in the system's biodiversity. As in other ecosystems, the sustainability of grasslands depends on recognizing the value of their diversity. It is through its resource base that the system can maintain the flexibility it needs and the potential for sustained use in the future.

6

Aquatic Ecosystems

....

Extractive exploitation

Aquatic ecosystems have provided food and other resources to various cultures for a very long time. For many societies, fish and other aquatic organisms are still a main source of food and income. Exploitation of aquatic ecosystems has been largely through extractive methods, mainly because these systems are much harder to manage than such closed systems as agriculture or livestock farming. In fact, it is difficult even to establish ownership of water resources.

One cannot routinely "fence" portions of water to keep target species within a limited area as is normally done on land. In oceans and open-sea environments, accurate locations are difficult to establish. Even in large lakes and rivers, it is seldom possible to keep an exploited species within a limited area or prevent others from catching it. Only in small lakes or streams or shallow coastal waters (especially bays, estuaries, and tidal zones) can ecosystems be controlled in any way.

There are cases, however — such as in Japan and other east Asian countries — where aquatic resource management is based on community use and claims are recognized by neighbouring communities. In these countries, fishing areas are often fenced off. Exploitation of controlled or artificial aquatic ecosystems has been an important activity since ancient times. Some agricultural systems in Asia (south China, for example) include intensive fish farming in carefully managed ponds. This type of aquaculture is frequently associated with rice production, which also requires careful management of water. Other areas of the world where the practice has been important include the Philippines and India.

Early fishing methods did not result in a significant reduction of fish stocks; thus, large aquatic ecosystems remained virtually unchanged by extractive activities. About the end of the 19th century, however, this situation changed dramatically when large fleets began fishing on an extensive scale in the more productive areas of the world.

Productivity of aquatic ecosystems is limited mainly by the amount of dissolved oxygen and some key nutrients, such as phosphorus and nitrogen. Oxygen concentration depends largely on the temperature of the water; higher levels are found in low-temperature environments. The more important nutrients in oceans and seas are carried from the adjacent continent by rivers, underwater streams, etc., or from the sea bottom through the upwelling of deeper, cooler waters. Finally, solar radiation contributes to productivity in aquatic ecosystems by increasing the potential for photosynthesis and primary production. This combination of factors is found on the Pacific coast of South America, in the northwestern Pacific, and on the Grand Banks in the North Atlantic, for example.

Recent improvements in fishing methods, including the widespread use of trawlers, draggers, spotter planes and helicopters, and directional radar to locate large schools of fish precisely, have made sustainable management of fish stocks difficult. In addition, fishing fleets from several countries have converged on the more accessible fishing zones, resulting in overfishing and subsequent decreases in the annual catch. Now, a vessel can tend up to four inexpensive nylon filament nets instead of one and freezing chambers can store hundreds of tonnes of fish, allowing the fleets to deplete large areas in a short time.

Agreements and controls have come too late; they are insufficient and not respected. Even with controls, fishermen frequently find ways to catch what they can before someone else does. Small fish of the target species are discarded because fishermen want the best price for their allowed quotas. Other species are also thrown away even though other fishermen might be interested in them. It is practically impossible to patrol all areas of the seas, and illegal nets are easy to hide. The result is widespread overfishing, far beyond the defined limits of sustainability. Many of the largest stocks of fish, such as those in the South American Pacific and the North Atlantic, have been exploited beyond their replacement potential. In 1990 and 1991, the Food and Agriculture Organization reported that the world catch had begun to decrease. "Fishermen are living off capital, consuming the resource that should yield their catch" (*Economist* 1994b).

The Peruvian fisheries

In Peruvian coastal waters, the main species sought was the Peruvian anchovy. To a large extent, exploitation of this species was a result of extensive fishing by newly formed Peruvian fishing companies or concessions awarded by the Peruvian government to foreign fishing fleets from Japan, Russia, and Poland, among others. The annual catch increased quickly, reaching a maximum of 13 million tonnes in 1970. In 1973, a crisis occurred, and the volume of the catch dropped to less than 2 million tonnes. Since then, it has remained below 5 million tonnes (Table 3).

North Atlantic fisheries

In the North Atlantic, large-scale fishing was concentrated in the North Sea, along the Norwegian coast, in the coastal areas of Iceland and Greenland, and on the Grand Banks off the North American coast. These fisheries are based mainly on cod, herring, and other species that are not for human consumption, such as Norway pout, capelin, blue whiting, and sand eels. Overfishing caused a decrease in cod and herring catches beginning in the late 1960s and continuing through the 1970s. The large cod catches of about 3.3 million tonnes in 1970 plummeted

Table 3. World production of main commercial fish species.

Species	Production (tonnes per year)	Location
Alaska pollack	4.89	N Pacific
Yellowfin tuna	1.01	Pacific, Atlantic, and Indian oceans
Club mackerel	1.17	Pacific
Peruvian anchovy	4.02	SE Pacific
South American pilchard	4.19	SE Pacific
Chilean jack mackerel	3.89	SE Pacific
Atlantic cod	1.33	N Atlantic
Atlantic herring	1.36	N Atlantic
European pilchard	1.97	Mediterranean
Capefin	1.25	NE Atlantic
Japanese pilchard	3.71	NW Pacific
Skipjack tuna	1.66	Pacific and Indian oceans

Source: *Economist* (1994b).

to 2.2 million tonnes by 1978. Herring yields dropped to 0.8 million tonnes in 1978 from 2.6 million tonnes in 1970. The trend continued unabated throughout the 1980s, resulting in the current critical situation that forced governments to ban fishing in some of the main fisheries, such as the Grand Banks (see box 4).

Other world fisheries

The north Pacific is also an important fishing area. The continental shelves are narrow, but catches of pelagic species — mackerel, anchovy, sardine, and herring — are large. The annual harvest in this area reached a maximum of 22 million tonnes, mainly from the northwestern sector.

The main countries fishing in the north Pacific are Japan, China, and, to a lesser degree, Canada, United States, Russia, and North and South Korea. Japan has more than 1 500 fishing ports, and the total annual catch exceeds 10 million tonnes, of which about 20% comes from coastal fisheries. About half of the protein in the Japanese diet is derived from fish.

4.
The Grand Banks

Located on a shallow continental shelf, the Grand Banks receive a rich supply of nutrients and oxygen in the cold Labrador current. This area contains one of the largest fish stocks of the Atlantic Ocean, and fleets from all over the world have been fishing here regularly for centuries. The intensive harvest, mainly of cod, increased in the 1960s. In 1968, vessels from West Germany, the Soviet Union, Spain, and several other fishing countries, as well as Canada, were trawling in the area for cod and other commercial species. The total catch obtained from the Grand Banks was nearly 1 million tonnes of fish per year.

After 1977, activity decreased somewhat with the extension of the territorial waters and economic zone claimed by Canada and the United States to 200 miles (320 kilometres) from the coast. However, international exploitation beyond that boundary continued. In addition, French fishing fleets regularly visited the area by taking advantage of the French jurisdiction around the islands of Saint Pierre and Miquelon in the Gulf of St Lawrence.

During the 1970s and early 1980s, fishing by Canadian and American boats was still intense. In Canada, fishing plants were established and fishers were encouraged to buy bigger boats; even the government set up two off-shore trawling operations. Along with the competition from US and French fishers, cod resources were nearly depleted.

Other factors also played a role, such as the suspension of the seal hunt, which dramatically increased the number of seals feeding on fish. In any case, the equilibrium of the ecosystem was upset by human intervention, with serious social, economic, and environmental implications.

The Sea of Okhotsk fisheries have been exploited intensively for several decades, especially for pollack, the most important commercial fish in the region (Bird 1993). Traditionally, Russia and Japan have been the primary countries fishing in the Okhotsk. Currently, pollack stocks are seriously threatened. The fish is now unavailable, even where it was a traditional food, such as in the Russian cities of the Far East.

Overfishing has occurred because of a lack of control. Only very low catches have been reported to the Pacific Ocean Research Institute for Fisheries and Oceanography. At a meeting in Vladivostok in September 1993, requests for a moratorium from Russia, Japan, and the

United States were rejected by the Polish and South Korean delega-
tions. It is widely believed, however, that the main cause of the
depleted stock is overfishing by the "joint ventures" established between
Russian and foreign enterprises.

Growth in the world's fisheries has stopped. From 1950 to 1988,
the annual growth in fish catches was 4%. In the following 4 years
(1988–1992), it fell at a rate of 0.8% per year (Brown 1993).

The decrease in catches was partly offset by the opening of new
fisheries, such as those in the southern Atlantic. The growth or persistence of artisanal fisheries, which are much less devastating than factory
fishing fleets, has also helped to stabilize production figures.

Today, world production stands at 87 million tonnes per year
(World Bank et al. 1993); another 13 million tonnes per year is contributed by aquaculture, bringing the annual total to about 100 million
tonnes. Of this harvest, about 70% is consumed by people and about
30% is used for oil extraction and animal feed. Demand is continuing to
grow, but natural fisheries are nearing their limits of sustainability.
Catches in the main fisheries will continue to decrease. Even in the face
of disaster, however, greed may impel some to further expand fishing
activities until they become uneconomic or until global awareness of
the problem forces the implementation of appropriate controls.

Overfishing is not the only problem affecting aquatic ecosystems.
Water quality in the oceans is affected by polluted influxes from coastal,
industrial, urban, and farming areas. As a result, in some coastal zones,
important fish stocks have been reduced or eliminated by pollution and
habitat degradation, and others cannot be consumed safely because of
the concentration of contaminants in their tissues.

In some coastal countries, marine pollution has become a nightmare. This is the case in most of the Mediterranean Sea, where a continuous outflow of wastewater effluent and spills has drastically damaged
the natural ecosystems of the Adriatic and Ligurian seas and the eastern
and western edges of the Mediterranean. Other marine environments
where pollution is seriously affecting the aquatic ecosystems include the
Black Sea, the North Sea, the northwestern Atlantic, the Japan Sea,
the China Sea, the Persian Gulf, and the Red Sea. In the coastal areas

of Florida, the ecosystem is close to collapse as a result of repeated algal blooms, which are systematically affecting local fish hatcheries (Dewar 1993). Similar phenomena have been observed in Malaysia and Brazil. Undoubtedly, the rapidly spreading degradation of oceanic and marine water bodies is a new and increasingly important factor contributing to the worldwide decline in fish populations.

The future of fish production

The future of the extractive fishing industry has become less and less promising. Almost all of the 200 world fisheries are dependant on a few commercial species that are being fully exploited. However, the seas contain 15 thousand species, 99% of which are not used commercially. Although it is usually impractical to envisage commercial exploitation of these noncommercial species, a different approach — such as using artisanal methods or multispecific commercial fishing systems — might be possible to maintain catch values (although probably not the volumes).

Even with such adjustments, however, it appears that extractive production will not be able to satisfy the growing need for seafood, particularly in developing countries. Despite declines in the production capacity of the fishing industry, worldwide consumption of fish has continued to grow and even accelerate, and this trend is not expected to change in the near future. There is widespread agreement that seafood contains some essential nutrients that are not present in land animals or plants, and that its unsaturated fats make it a healthy source of protein (by lowering cholesterol levels in the blood, etc.).

By the year 2000, the demand for fish products will probably increase by another 30 million tonnes. It will be difficult to meet this demand when production from most large-scale fisheries is reaching its limit or decreasing. Locally, some increases can be expected in artisanal fisheries, but these will not meet world demands.

The growth of aquaculture

During the last few years, mainly as a result of global trends and demands for seafood, large investments at international and national levels have been directed toward aquaculture, particularly in some (mostly developing) countries where conditions are favourable (adequate temperature, abundance of nutrients, and inexpensive labour and operating costs). About 12 million tonnes of seafood per year is produced through aquaculture, and the industry is growing at a rate of about 10% per year (*Economist* 1994b). Of this harvest, about 70% is finfish species, 25% is shellfish, and 5% is shrimp. Some of the most important species of finfish produced by aquaculture are carp, tilapia, salmon, and trout.

The "artificial" production of various sea species is introducing profound changes in the economic structure of the fishing sector. Shrimp consumption is satisfied by a few Third World suppliers. Some countries, such as Ecuador and the Philippines, have become large producers because of their strategic location. In Ecuador, the value of shrimp exports to the United States, Canada, and other countries increased from $56.8 million in 1980 to $491.3 million in 1991. In 1993, 150 thousand people were involved in catching shrimp larvae and in shrimp farming; this is several times the number of people involved in artisanal (50 thousand) or industrial fisheries (2 600).

Aquaculture may have a strong impact on the aquatic environment; for example, water is contaminated by organic matter and food chains are disturbed. Increased aquaculture activity may also affect aquatic ecosystems by adding to existing overfishing and contamination problems. Meeting world demands for seafood through aquaculture will mean increasing annual production from 12 million tonnes to 35 or 40 million tonnes in 6 or 7 years. This may be very stressful for the ecosystems where aquaculture is carried out and may be unsustainable in the medium and long terms.

Protecting diversity and sustainable production

The future of aquatic ecosystems will ultimately depend on the sustainability of production strategies. Natural aquatic ecosystems, like any other natural system, can be exploited for a long period only by carefully controlled methods that do not affect stock levels and biodiversity in the systems. If adequate controls are not enforced, worldwide demands for fish will not be met and continued degradation of aquatic ecosystems can be expected. However, rational management strategies, such as the promotion of local artisanal fisheries rather than large-scale, monospecific commercial fishing or diversification of consumption, may lead to sustained production and even some increases.

Substantial expansion of aquaculture activities will be necessary to keep up with the growth in demand for its products. If aquaculture strategies are based on conservation of natural environments, the biodiversity of ecosystems, and stocks, aquaculture may become another effective tool for feeding the population of the world without diminishing the value of its systems.

Management of estuarine environments

About 150 million people live on or near estuarine bodies of water on five continents. In North America, major estuaries are associated with the St Lawrence and Hudson rivers; in South America, the Río de la Plata (see box 5), the Guayas in Ecuador, the Amazon estuary in Brazil, and the Orinoco in Venezuela. In Africa, because there are few well-developed coastal plains, estuaries are rare; only the Senegal, Congo, and Niger rivers have large estuarine ecosystems near their outlets to the Atlantic Ocean. In Asia, important estuaries occur in China (the Yangtze and Yellow rivers), India (the Ganges), and Indochina (the Mekong).

Estuarine regions represent the outlet of agricultural, fishing, commercial, and navigation activities in extensive areas far greater than the estuaries themselves. Even when they remain undisturbed by human activity, estuaries are fragile environments, experiencing frequent changes in salinity, sediment load, nutrient levels, and other physico-chemical characteristics. When human influence is added to the equation, the fragility of the ecosystems increases, and degradation can result in irreversible loss of production potential and biodiversity.

5.
The case of Río de la Plata

The Río de la Plata ecosystem is typical of the world's estuarine environments. The widest estuarine body in Latin America, it sustains a broad spectrum of valuable species, some of which are unique. Fish found in the typical estuarine zone are croaker (or corvina), flounder, flatfish, lacha, lisa (*Mugil platanus* and *M. brasiliensis*), white pargo, merluzas (*Merluccius merluccius*), and brótola (*Urophycis brasiliensis*). In the freshwater environment, species include sábalos (*Prochilodus lineatus*), bagre (*Thamdia sapo* and *Pimelodus clarias*), surubí (*Psuedoplatystoma* spp.), dorado (*Salminus maxillosus*), and patí (*Luciopimelodus pati*).

The Río de la Plata coastal zones are fished on a regular basis by several communities, mainly for hake and croaker. Hake, squid, tuna, anchovy, and several other species are obtained in deep waters, where the estuarine influence is less important, by commercial fleets owned by many small, medium, and a few large enterprises.

Croakers, which are among the most important commercial species in the Río de la Plata region, are mainly found in the heart of the estuarine zone near Montevideo. They are exploited by artisanal fishermen and the coastal commercial fleet. In 1992, 25 thousand tonnes of croaker was harvested.

The main fishing communities are located in Pajas Blancas, Puerto del Buceo, and San Luis. The commercial fleets are based in the ports of Montevideo and Buenos Aires. Currently, 20 thousand people are employed directly or indirectly in the estuarine fishing industry in both countries. Commercial fishing is geared toward export markets, whereas artisanal fisheries satisfy local consumption.

Recent developments in the Río de la Plata highlight the fragility of the estuarine ecosystem. First, episodes of widespread fish mortality are becoming more common in the region; millions of fish die for no apparent reason. Second, contamination from coastal sources seems to be increasing. At least 15 million people and 50 thousand industries are located along the shores; more than half the industries emit polluting effluent into the environment and practically no waste treatment is available. This pollution is worsened by the outflow of fluvial water loaded with sediment, fertilizers, and pesticides from the farming areas surrounding Montevideo and, to a lesser degree, Buenos Aires.

The outflow of these contaminants, together with overfishing or inadequate fishing practices, may jeopardize the sustainability of the estuarine resources, along with the viability of the artisanal and commercial fisheries. An unwanted by-product of the contamination process may be a decline in the quality of the fish, which may affect the health of the fish-consuming population.

Because of their complexity and the continuous changes they experience, estuarine ecosystems require a much more careful and thoughtful management approach than other larger or more stable bodies of water. Although these systems occupy an important geographic "niche" in populated areas, no specific methods have been developed to address the issue of their sustainable management. The main elements to be considered are the following:

- The pattern of normal changes that takes place on a regular basis as a result of the interaction of the coastal and fluvial regimes;

- Periodic, catastrophic natural events, such as floods, hurricanes, unusually high tides, abrupt changes in salinity, or extreme variations in sediment load; and

- Anthropogenic influences, such as contamination, fishing, infrastructure in coastal areas, and changes in neighbouring basins.

In addition to these physical and biological factors, estuarine management is also limited by social, economic, political, and cultural elements that can also affect the human environment in which management decisions must be made. To address the issue properly, it is necessary both to gather the necessary scientific and traditional knowledge and to develop an adequate method for formulating and implementing appropriate policies and strategies.

7

Managing Planetary Thirst

....

Some basic facts

Most of the world's water is stored in the oceans (97.39%) and in glaciers and ice sheets (2.01%). A large part of the remainder is contained in geological formations (0.54%). Only about 0.06% occurs as surface water, of which more than half is salty, making it unpotable. Therefore, available fresh water constitutes less than 0.02% of the hydrosphere. Of surface fresh water, 95% is stored in lakes. Flowing water represents only about 0.001% of the water on the planet (Bethemont 1980). However, this volume of flowing water is more than enough to satisfy all human needs now and in the near future.

Every year, 496 thousand cubic **kilometres** of water falls as precipitation — that is about 100 thousand cubic metres per person per year. If the annual precipitation was spread evenly over the planet, it would amount to about 973 millimetres. However, only 25% of this total falls on the continents. Asia receives the most (28%), despite its low average precipitation of 696 millimetres per year. South America, with less than half the area, receives almost as much (25%) because of its higher average precipitation (1 564 millimetres per year). Africa's average precipitation is similar to Asia's; North America's is slightly lower (645 millimetres per year). Assuming that the volume of stored groundwater is unchanged, the volume of water lost to evaporation from the land masses is as high as 84% of the total precipitation in Africa, 67% in Australia, and 62% in North America. In Asia and South America, evaporation loss accounts for 60% of the fallen water; in Europe, 57%. Only in Antarctica is the rate considerably smaller at 17%.

If we restrict our calculations to precipitation falling on the continents and subtract the amount lost to evaporation (about 60%), over 80 thousand cubic metres would be available for each person annually. Per-capita need varies from place to place, but generally does not exceed 1 cubic metre per day. These figures show that availability of water for human use does not relate to its volume. Rather, it depends on many other factors that we identify and characterize in this chapter.

Hydrographic basins

Hydrographic basins are natural units made up of the various terrestrial environments through which water moves toward a given outlet. In that sense, hydrographic basins can be defined as the upstream territories of a lake or stream. Basins are complex; they include both surface and underground water. These two categories of water are closely interrelated and must be considered together. The main components of a typical basin are watersheds, a hydrographic network, and groundwater systems.

The three parts of a hydrographic basin are interconnected: watersheds receive precipitation, which infiltrates groundwater systems or flows toward valleys, forming streams. Part of the groundwater can go back into the streams, and water from the streambeds often recharges the underlying aquifers. Some water may reenter the atmosphere through evaporation and fall again on the watershed, closing the cycle. By and large, however, the system is open because most basins exit toward the sea or other major water body. The outlet of the basin is also an outlet for sediments, dissolved salts, and contaminants.

The geomorphic water cycle

Surface waters may occur in a complex array of hydrologic features and systems, including streams, lakes, swamps, and other flowing or lentic water bodies. Surface water bodies are fed from three main sources: instantaneously from rainstorms and subsequent runoff; from springs (groundwater discharge); and from the melting of ice and snow.

In tropical and temperate arid climates, streams are mainly fed through runoff. Precipitation falls on bare soils, little or no infiltration occurs, and the water flows downhill into river valleys. Rivers in arid areas have irregular flow patterns and may suffer catastrophic floods and droughts. In humid climates, the opposite occurs. Soils are covered by vegetation, and rainwater is intercepted by leaves and branches. Most of the water evaporates or infiltrates the soil and only a small fraction remains as surface runoff. Underground, the water moves through geological formations, reappearing as springs next to streams, lakes, or swamps.

Thus, in humid climates most of the water comes from springs, whereas in arid areas the supply of water to the natural surface systems is related to runoff processes. In addition, as a result of higher evaporation rates and the presence of salts in the soil, water in arid climates tends to contain a higher concentration of dissolved solids; in humid environments the opposite is true.

Difficulty of managing international hydrographic basins

Hydrographic basins, both on the surface and underground, do not respect national boundaries; nor are national borders arranged around water systems. The sharing of water resources is common throughout the world. In some cases, conflicts may develop, and water issues may become important factors in international politics.

Some hydrographic basins, even a few large ones, are mainly or entirely within a single country; for example, the Yangtze River in China and the Mississippi River in the United States. Hydrographic basins are more frequently shared by two or more countries, however, making agreement on management strategies difficult.

Water supply and options

Despite the enormous volume of fresh water that circulates through the continents annually — easily enough to satisfy the needs of humankind for centuries — many people around the world do not have access to this vital liquid. There are several reasons for this. First, although water is abundant, fresh water only exists in large volumes in small areas of the planet (the lower reaches of rivers, large lakes, and high-yield aquifers). Second, available fresh water is not always fit for human consumption, sometimes because of natural causes, but more often as a result of anthropogenic degradation. Third, not all water sources are renewed at a sufficiently high rate to be suitable for long-term use. Finally, water demand is concentrated in a few densely populated areas, which do not necessarily coincide with the sites of greatest availability.

In brief, good-quality fresh water available in sufficient volumes and in a sustainable manner to meet the needs of populations and productive activities is not easily found. Increasingly, it has become a limiting factor in demographic and economic growth.

Water use and overuse

Water is the most widely used substance on Earth: it is needed in homes for washing, cooking, and drinking; it is used by industries as a raw material, for cooling or washing, to make possible certain processes; it is required for farming and for many other purposes. Farmers are responsible for more than 80% of the world's water consumption. Of the remaining 20%, about half is consumed domestically and the rest is used by industries and for other activities.

These figures reflect only the water that is actually used, however. Additional large volumes of natural water are only "affected" by human action. Good-quality river or lake water is often rendered unfit for use by the return of untreated or insufficiently treated wastewater into its environment. The volume of natural water that is affected by human activities is enormous and difficult to quantify. In all likelihood, the volume of degraded water is probably on at least the same order of magnitude as all the water used worldwide, and may be substantially greater.

Another anthropogenic cause of water degradation or, at least, decreased availability relates to inappropriate soil management on slopes. Inadequate farming or grazing practices cause soil erosion, and runoff water carries agricultural fertilizers and pesticides. In such "overused" areas, water flow is often concentrated over a short period, causing flooding and making optimum use of the water resource more difficult. Floodwater is usually loaded with suspended particles that not only lower its quality but also clog intake mechanisms at filtration plants, making its treatment more costly and difficult.

Anthropogenic impact on water systems

In ancient times, hydrographic basins evolved naturally at variable paces depending on climatic, geologic, and biologic factors. Since the beginning of history, however, societies have introduced other factors. Agriculture, raising cattle, logging, excavation of quarries, and construction of artificial structures have had an effect on hydrodynamics throughout the planet. The growth of the world's population, particularly after the industrial revolution, has gradually increased the impact of these factors as widespread modifications were made to the land surface. Anthropogenic effects have been particularly intense since the urban revolution of the 20th century. Overpopulation in many rural areas and the development of large cities with populations in the millions have created a concentrated and growing demand for water.

During this century, the amount of water used for agricultural, domestic, industrial, and other purposes has continued to increase; dams have been built, wells drilled, and water taken from natural sources at an unprecedented rate. "Used water" of lower quality is being returned to the environment, causing widespread degradation of streams, lakes, and aquifers.

Vulnerability of water resources

The vulnerability of water resources to contamination varies from place to place. Generally, it depends on volume. Large rivers are less vulnerable than smaller rivers. The same rationale applies to lakes, although they are more susceptible than rivers because of their slower rate of renewal. However, surface water sources are relatively easy to clean up once a commitment is made to do so.

Groundwater, on the other hand, is less vulnerable than surface water in the short term. It takes longer for contaminants to find their way into deep aquifers. In some cases, they may even be protected by impermeable layers of soil or rock. However, groundwater reservoirs can be polluted easily by contamination of their recharge areas or inappropriate drilling operations. When this happens, the damage may be difficult and expensive to correct. In most cases, contaminated aquifers cannot be used for a long time and, in some cases, they may never again be suitable for any practical purpose.

Water problems in densely populated areas

The industrial revolution resulted in gradual growth of urban centres, with the populations of London, New York, and Paris exceeding 1 million by the beginning of the 20th century. Today, as many as 200 cities have populations over 1 million and more than 20 have over 10 million people.

In most cases, water resources were abundant when these cities were first established. Many drew their water supplies from nearby rivers or lakes, which were more than sufficient. Where surface fresh water was not available, cities used easily accessible underground aquifers. In fact, in almost all cases, it was the presence of water resources that made the development of the new cities possible.

In cases of both spontaneous and planned development, however, almost without exception, the location of cities was not chosen based on anticipation of the growth that has taken place in many of the largest urban areas of the world. In the 18th and 19th centuries, most of today's largest cities would now be considered small or medium sized. By 1800, no city in the Americas had a population over 100 thousand.

For these levels of population, only relatively limited water resources were necessary. In the early 19th century, however, even small cities had poorly developed water-supply systems. For this reason, per-capita consumption levels were much lower than they are today.

During the late 19th and 20th centuries, many cities grew to become megalopolises. At the same time, their need for water increased dramatically: in some cases, per-capita consumption increased to 600 litres per year. Large cities consume large volumes of water. Los Angeles, Mexico City, and Tokyo — three of the world's largest cities — use 50 to 150 cubic metres of water every second. These volumes may seem impressive; however, they are relatively minor compared with the flow of our planet's largest rivers. The efflux of the Amazon into the Atlantic Ocean is about 150 thousand cubic metres per second, 2 thousand times the consumption rate of the largest megacity of the world. The Congo flows at an average rate of 60 thousand cubic metres per second, and many other rivers, such as the Paraná, Yangtze, and Mississippi, deliver over 5 thousand cubic metres of water to the sea or coastal estuaries every second.

This apparent overabundance of water does not reflect reality, however. The Amazon and the Congo are not typical because a significant portion of their basins lies in high rainfall areas. Many other rivers with large basins (such as the Nile and the Niger) have considerably lower flow volumes. On average, much less water is actually available. The numbers given here reflect the flow at the mouth of these rivers, where it is greatest. In other stretches of the rivers and in their tributaries, the flow is much lower in relation to the size of the upstream basin and local rainfall. Also, not many large cities or densely populated areas are located at the mouth or in the lower reaches of the largest rivers or their tributaries where water flow is at its maximum.[7] As a result, the actual surface water resources available for cities and densely populated areas are much smaller than they would be if the cities were ideally located.

Many cities that are at the mouths of large rivers (such as Georgetown in Guyana and Montevideo in Uruguay) cannot use the water directly because of its brackish quality, which is caused by invading seawater during the dry season. Some cities are close to divides, so

---

[7] Exceptions are Bengal on the lower Ganges and Brahmaputra rivers, Shanghai and neighbouring areas next to the Yangtze, and Ho Chi Minh City and other high-density areas near the mouth of the Mekong River.

available water is limited (São Paulo and Madrid), or next to relatively small streams (Los Angeles and Lima). Available resources frequently cannot meet the growing needs of neighbouring metropolitan areas.

Despite potential problems, at the beginning of the 20th century, the world's main urban centres were managing to survive using their nearby water resources without major problems of scarcity. During the 20th century, however, the situation changed radically. Cities that formerly had populations of 50 to 100 thousand have grown to urban areas of 10 to 15 million, housing as many or more people in surrounding areas. At current rates of growth, or even with some stabilization in the near future, by the beginning of the next decade there will be several megalopolises with over 15 million people.

In many of these megacities, local water resources have been exhausted or were degraded many decades ago, and water authorities have been forced to turn to neighbouring hydrographic basins or aquifers. As a result, the cost of water has risen considerably, although in most cases it is somewhat disguised in national budgets. Often, urban water-supply accounts list only operational costs, investments are financed at the national level, and, in some cases, even replacement costs are not fully considered.

When cities do not pay the full price of their water, however, someone else does. In many countries, large cities are being subsidized by the population at large, including taxpayers in small towns and rural people who do not benefit from the waterworks.

Continuing growth of large urban areas will make the problem more acute. New sources of water can only be farther away or deeper; tapping them will require more costly dams, conduction systems, storage structures, distribution networks, and treatment plants. A successful strategy will have to be aimed at redefining management strategies not only to increase supply, but also to reduce demand, unnecessary consumption, and losses. A longer term solution will require reexamination of the "constant growth" development paradigms that are the cause of unsustainability in current systems. A new approach may be required in which water consumption will be related to its distribution and availability and where rational and equitable demand policies are given priority over additional spending and waste.

Power generation

Water overuse is often related to the need to generate power. In Armenia, historical Lake Sevan is gradually being drained by the Razdan River power plants to produce badly needed electricity. The power plants were built in the 1940s and the water levels at that time were 20 metres higher that they are today. The lake is now eutrophic and its area is rapidly decreasing. In addition, because of the recent conflict between Armenia and Azerbaijan, Armenia was cut off from its oil supplies (which used to come from Azerbaijan) and electricity production in the Razdan plants has increased, accelerating the process of degradation (Gray 1993). This is yet another demonstration of how wars and conflicts between nations can destroy the environment.

Use of groundwater

In many areas, the volume of groundwater resources may be much greater than that of surface water; in terms of usable fresh water, the difference may be several orders of magnitude. However, the amount of groundwater available should not be measured by its volume, but in terms of its rate of renewal. When groundwater resources are used faster than they are replaced, water levels in aquifers drop, pumping costs increase, and sooner or later the resource is depleted.

Judging aquifers in terms of their renewability, available volumes of water are about equal to or less than those of surface resources. In addition, groundwater availability and urban populations do not necessarily coincide. Some large aquifers are located in sparsely populated areas or where they are not needed because sufficient surface water exists; at the same time, many large urban areas have very little groundwater in close proximity. Despite these limitations, the use of groundwater offers many advantages:

- It is less vulnerable to contamination;
- It usually does not require treatment to make is suitable for drinking;

- It can be exploited using a modular approach with smaller capital investment and local participation;

- It does not require large, sophisticated distribution systems; and

- It does not need expensive storage structures — it is already stored underground.

Although groundwater may be a feasible alternative for providing water to urban areas, particular care must be taken to protect it from degradation by outside sources and from overuse. As mentioned above, although aquifers are less vulnerable to contamination, when they are affected, the damage may be irreversible.

The particular problems of coastal cities

A common limitation to water supplies in coastal areas is the intrusion of brackish water into the lower reaches of rivers. This has forced cities such as London (on the Thames) and Guayaquil (on the Guayas) to relocate their water-supply intake farther upstream.

Coastal cities depending on nearby aquifers for water have also experienced problems with saltwater intrusion as a result of drawing too much water from the underground resource. Seawater enters the aquifer when the piezometric level drops below a certain point.

Many of these cities — such as Recife, Brazil; Calcutta, India; Dakar, Senegal; Georgetown, Guyana; and Maracaibo, Venezuela — have had to pipe water from distant rivers or groundwater sources. Others, on salty rivers or estuaries, have turned to nearby freshwater tributaries. New York, for example, was forced to use groundwater because the Hudson River is brackish. Currently, its water supply comes from upstream reservoirs. Montevideo, Uruguay, cannot depend on the Río de la Plata, which has an average salinity of 10‰ (per thousand), but gets its water from intakes in the Santa Lucia River, a tributary of the Río de la Plata, 30 kilometres upstream of its mouth and 15 to 30 kilometres from the city.

Some coastal cities are not close to a river, especially those located on karstic or volcanic sites (for example, Djakarta, Indonesia; Manila, Philippines; Miami, United States; Havana, Cuba; and Mérida,

Mexico). These cities rely entirely on groundwater for their water supplies.

Other limitations

The growing contamination of surface water — resulting from a lack of wastewater treatment — is gradually becoming a central issue. In many densely populated areas, all types of wastewater find their way into the natural water systems. For example, there is a $3 billion plan to clean up the Tietê River in São Paulo. However, it is unlikely to be carried out before the year 2000 and there are indications from international and local environmental NGOs that, because of special interests and constraints, the project may never even approach its final goal.

In summary, there are two basic limitations affecting the water supplies of cities and densely populated areas of the world. One is the inappropriate location of cities in relation to existing natural water resources; the other is the growing degradation of those resources.

The demand side of the issue

Water-supply problems are not alone, however. In fact, the water problem has two sides: the availability of resources — or the supply side — and water-consumption issues — or the demand side. Many water-supply problems would not exist, or would be much less acute, if more sustainable policies and strategies were formulated and implemented that better accounted for the demand side.

In most countries and cities, consumption is actually much greater than what is required to serve human activities. Wastage takes place at all stages in water systems: leakage from pipelines, wasteful attitudes encouraged by a lack of metering or inadequate pricing policies, inappropriate water-appliance technology, etc. To improve the situation, this waste must be reduced through improved management strategies.

In most urban areas, water shortages could be prevented for many years with better system maintenance and appropriate metering and pricing policies. Such a strategy would be more economical in terms of both time and money and would reduce the deleterious effects on natural water systems. However, very few cities in the world have moved toward such a sustainable approach to water management. This lack of action is related to the types of development models that have been adopted in most countries.

Sustainability and equity in urban areas

To solve urban water-supply problems, management strategies must weigh required investments against returns within a framework of sustainability and equity. For every densely populated area of the world, there are several possible sustainable and equitable water-supply options. Usually, once sustainability and equity are assured, the main criteria for choosing among the various alternatives would be the financial costs of the proposed systems.

Many other factors enter the equation, however. Some relate to the concept of sustainability. First, water-supply systems should not affect the sustainability of the water resources themselves (that is, the rate of use should not be higher than the rate of renewal, and the quality should not be lowered). Second, the sustainability concept includes protecting other natural resources in the region (fluvial or lacustrine ecosystems should be protected).

In addition to ecological sustainability, water systems must be socially sustainable. The implementation of any water system involves socioeconomic implications, not only from the perspective of satisfying the needs of all the population in an equitable way, but also from other points of view. Establishing water services creates employment, promotes some types of industries, and even affects other urban strategies (for example, the availability of water will stimulate the development of some neighbourhoods over others).

Water and models for development in urban areas

Even with sustainable approaches to water management, population growth in many areas exceeds the potential of local, natural systems. In those cases, the problem does not lie in the resources, but in the development models that have flourished throughout the world during the last few decades and, in fact, the last few centuries. It is clear that megacities are not sustainable entities. One wonders, for example, about the future of Mexico City, with 20 million people and still growing. Water is becoming insufficient and huge amounts of money and energy are being spent to produce larger and larger volumes of water, but the city and surrounding urban centres (Toluca, Puebla, Cuernavaca, and Cuautla) are still growing. The development model of Mexico City must be reviewed, growth should be curtailed, and the country's economy and management system must be decentralized. If these things are done in an intelligent manner, there is a real possibility that the water problem will disappear, or at least be significantly reduced.

In the Philippines and Thailand, the increasing centralization of the economies in two megacities is not sustainable. Neither Manila nor Bangkok is located in an area that can accommodate an urban population exceeding 10 million without irreversible deterioration of the environment, including the water supplies. The problem is also apparent in Brazil. Hydrologically, São Paulo was in the wrong place to start with, and time and further growth of the city have worsened the situation. A new model requiring the relocation of some of the city's activities may be the only long-term solution to many of its serious problems, including its water supply. The same arguments could be applied to many other cities of the world; Tehran, Bombay, Dakar, Kinshasa, Lagos, and Lima, to various degrees, present similar problems.

Irrigated agriculture: one of the largest water users

In most countries, it is not urban populations that require the largest volumes of water, but irrigation. Irrigated farming uses an enormous amount of water, especially because areas that require watering to grow crops are normally located where evaporation rates are high, and this is exacerbated by the type of crops planted, some of which have high transpiration rates.

On 1 hectare of irrigated rice, for example, as much as 20 thousand cubic metres of water may evaporate every year. Even for less-demanding crops, irrigated farms use as much water for each hectare, on average, as 40 urban homes. For this reason, irrigated agriculture can be

In areas where water is very scarce, irrigation systems — such as the drip-irrigation system shown here (near Abu Dhabi, United Arab Emirates) — can be very efficient.

competitive only if crops of high market value are grown or where the price of water is very low.

Frequently, the low price of water for irrigation does not reflect actual costs. In some irrigated zones, water is obtained from systems in which the cost of expensive dams or other waterworks has not been factored into its price. The artificially low cost of water allows the development or persistence of irrigated farming in areas where it would otherwise be economically unfeasible. In those cases, farming only survives because it is being subsidized by the institution or agency that built or financed the waterworks and is not passing along the cost to the water users.

In many cases, the capital investment was financed by a loan to a national government and is being repaid by society at large. In California, for example, large hydroworks on the Colorado River and elsewhere were financed by the federal government. In Mexico, as well, the investment needs of most irrigation districts, as well as a considerable part of the pumping costs, are or were supported by the federal government.

Defining water strategies

One of the pressing problems facing those developing strategies for the future relates to the allocation of water to the often competing areas of irrigated farming and urban use. Farmers use far more water than urban dwellers (even when large water-consuming industries are considered).

For this reason, the competitiveness of agricultural activities is closely related to the cost of water. Expensive water can exclude the farmer from the market. Urban dwellers can afford to pay more per unit of water because the cost of aquiring the water is shared by many more individuals and enterprises and because they use much less water on a per-capita basis.

In the competition between farmers and cities, the cities tend to have the upper hand. In some cases, this may be to the detriment of traditional farming activities by many small farmers who depend on irrigation (such as in Egypt). In other cases, speculative water policies result in water being taken from small farmers or indigenous communities and provided to large companies for commercial production (for example, the water transfer from Owens Valley to the lower valleys in California).

For this reason, it is necessary when defining water strategies to take into account all the elements of the equation.

- How much water is available?
- Who needs it the most?
- What share should be provided to each user?
- Who has priority?
- What makes the most sense economically?

Finally, these concerns must be answered within the framework of sound development models in which quality of life and sustainable use of resources are the main priorities. Use of water resources will be optimal and the water situation will be addressed satisfactorily only when sustainable social and environmental models are properly defined and adopted.

Water issues throughout the world

Water has always been a central element in the history of humankind and its use has frequently had profound social, economic, and political implications. Policies and decision-making in this field can have a great impact on the future of countries and societies. There are many examples in which conflicts over water have been a determining factor in the evolution of countries and societies. The following pages will cover some important or representative basins, illustrating some of the key water issues with environmental, social, and geopolitical implications.

The Amazon basin

The Amazon basin, covering 6.157 million square kilometres, is one of the largest river basins in the world. It is shared by seven countries: about two-thirds of the basin (4 million square kilometres) is in Brazil, nearly 1 million square kilometres lies in Peru, 825 thousand square kilometres in Bolivia, and the rest in Venezuela, Ecuador, Colombia, and Guyana.

The region is characterized by a high annual rainfall — averaging over 2 thousand millimetres — falling during two rainy seasons separated by drier periods. The vegetation is mainly dense rain forest, including extensive wetlands (almost 600 thousand square kilometres). The Amazon region is also home to some of the world's largest and most diverse ecosystems.

Because the basin is sparsely populated (25 million people, mainly living in the highlands and on the slopes of the Andes, with a density of only four people per square kilometre) and there is plenty of water available throughout, there have been few contentious issues related to the management of its resources. With the growing drive to build dams and the encroachment of mining operations, this situation is expected to change.

The population density of the rain forest itself is very small, as most settlements are situated along the rivers. The major cities of the basin are Manaus and Belém, with about 1.5 and 2 million people respectively; others include Iquitos in Peru and Santarém in Brazil. The river plays an important role in both transportation and fishing. Travel between communities of the basin has traditionally been by boat, although lately air travel has also become important. Land routes are few and, in the heart of the forest, almost nonexistent. Fishing has been one of the main subsistence activities of the population. Thus, contamination of the aquatic bioresources may represent not only a health hazard but also elimination of a source of food and income.

The region is also home to numerous indigenous micronations, which are well adapted to using the forest ecosystems. Although the destiny of these groups is closely linked with that of the water systems, decisions on basin management are usually made without any consideration of their point of view or interests. Land policies in Brazil have traditionally favoured the newly arrived occupant, who can prove possession by burning or logging the forest, rather than native groups who have lived on the land for many generations.

An important drive to occupy the region has been promoted by the building of dams, particularly by Brazil, which is the largest country in the area and has defined hydroelectric dam construction as a national strategy. There are plans to build dams at 43 sites on 13 rivers; they will have a generating capacity in excess of 70 thousand megawatts (Mougeot 1988). This "hydro-development" drive is to be concentrated in three river systems: the Xingu (32%), the Tocantins (20%), and the Madeira (15%). A number of dams have already been built, both on the Amazon and in neighbouring basins (such as the Paraná) with similar characteristics. In some cases, disastrous environmental and social effects have been observed (such as in the Tucurui impoundment on the lower Tocantins).

As a result of deforestation, hydrological regimes are already changing throughout the basin. Droughts and floods, formerly unknown, are taking place along many tributaries, and water quality is being affected by the increasing amount of effluent wastewaters entering the rivers from cities and mining operations.

Contamination from mining is related to the establishment of gold mines. Gold is extracted from ore using mercury or cyanide solutions. (In Brazil, the mercury technique is more common.) Both procedures damage the environment. Cyanide is highly poisonous and mercury becomes concentrated as it moves through the trophic chains and may reach toxic levels in some aquatic organisms that are consumed by the local people. In Japan, mercury poisoning affected the villagers of Minamata Bay in the 1950s, killing 1 382 people (Serril 1994). In the

Amazon, mercury pollution is particularly serious in the upper basins of
the Madeira, Tapajós, and Xingu rivers, and there are indications that
widespread poisoning may be taking place in some of the most polluted
areas. In the fishing community of Rainha, upstream of Itaituba on the
Tapajós, tests on the population showed mercury levels far in excess of
the 6 ppm maximum accepted by the World Health Organization.
Similar data were obtained in several other locations. In the Madeira
River basin, hazardous levels were found in the fish-eating Kayapo communities. Continuing mining operations are expected to increase the
environmental and human health effects of mercury contamination
further.

With deforestation and indiscriminate occupation, the apparently
invulnerable Amazon ecosystem is deteriorating, and this is not only
affecting its inhabitants but also the population of the world at large. It
will not be easy to address the many issues that are producing these
changes in the Amazon basin. New policies will be required in many
areas. Land allocation rules and recognition of the land rights of indigenous peoples should be reviewed. Migration to the region must also be
checked through adequate policies. The environmental and social
impact of hydro projects should be strictly and independently evaluated
to ensure that no further ecological destruction takes place. Finally, any
strategy will have to take into account not only the interests of the distant industrial metropolises but also the views of the people who live in
and suffer most from pollution of the Amazon: the indigenous nations
who have managed their land in a sustainable way for innumerable
generations.

The Rhine basin

In many ways, the Rhine basin is quite different from the Amazon. Its
population density is more than 120 times larger. In a relatively small
area, it accommodates more than 50 million people and drains a basin
located in seven countries: Austria, Belgium, France, Germany,
Luxembourg, the Netherlands, and Switzerland. Second, the river is
much smaller. It is only 1 320 kilometres long, and it drains a basin of
barely 185 thousand square kilometres. As the river flows from the Alps

to the North Sea, it crosses Switzerland, France, Germany, and the Netherlands. In this medium-sized basin, there are scores of large cities and some of the most densely populated areas on Earth (such as in Belgium and the Netherlands).

Not only does this river basin have a high population density, but it is also located in one of the most heavily industrialized regions of the world. Most of Germany's output, that of the Netherlands and Switzerland, and an important part of France's (Alsace and Lorraine) is produced or finds its way through the Rhine basin or its tributaries.

The intensive use of the basin has caused heavy contamination of the river, particularly in its lower reaches in Germany and the Netherlands. In 1985, pollutants in the Rhine at the border of the Netherlands and Germany were measured at the following levels: chloride, 1.1 million tonnes per year; phosphate, 3 500 tonnes per year; copper, 450 tonnes per year; cadmium, 10 tonnes per year; and benzpyrene, 1 600 kilograms per year (Maurits la Rivière 1989). The situation grew worse until 1980, but has improved more recently. Currently, the four countries bordering the river are cooperating under the Rhine Action Plan to address the problems of water quality in the river. One of the main strategies to be implemented includes improving industrial processes to reduce the number of contaminants entering the environment.

In addition, there has been a trend toward relocating some of the highly polluting industries to developing countries that have less-stringent environmental controls and cheaper labour (see Chapter 2).

The Nile basin

The Nile basin presents potential management problems that could become litigious issues between countries. The sources of the White Nile and its tributaries are in the African great lakes region, mainly in Uganda, but also in Kenya, Rwanda, and Tanzania. The Blue Nile and the Atbara, which are the main eastern tributaries, flow down from the Ethiopian highlands and provide not only a substantial portion of the water volume but also most of the sediment load. The middle course of the Nile, below the confluence of the White and the Blue tributaries, is in Sudan, and its lower course is in Egypt.

Because the river flows from humid areas (in the south) to increasingly dry areas (in the north), the downstream populations of northern Sudan and Egypt have depended on its water for centuries. In Egypt, where rainfall does not exceed 100 millimetres annually, the Nile is the only source of water. Egypt has a population of almost 60 million, concentrated chiefly along the banks of the Nile; most Egyptian towns and farms are densely packed in the 40 thousand square kilometres of the Nile's floodplain.

Any change in the Nile's regime could be a matter of life and death for the Egyptians. Currently, an international treaty ensures a minimum flow for Egypt at its southern border with Sudan. Sudan does not use its whole share of water; therefore, problems have not arisen yet.

A potential problem relates to the use of groundwater near the river. In northern Sudan and southern Egypt, the river crosses the Tertiary sedimentary basin of Nubian sandstone, which contains a large and relatively unstudied aquifer. An important portion of the water recharging this aquifer comes through infiltration from the Nile. Any large-scale use of the aquifer may result in a reduction in flow downstream. It will be difficult to control Sudan's use of the aquifer, as the relation between groundwater and surface water use has not been firmly established. Recent problems in multiethnic Sudan have prevented its inhabitants from increasing their use of water for irrigation.

Another potential problem for Nile communities is the proposed draining of the Sudd wetlands with the construction of a 360-kilometre canal (the Jonglei Canal) and other related waterworks. The Sudd region of southern Sudan is an area of high biodiversity that not only regulates the flow of the White Nile, reducing the risk of catastrophic floods and droughts, but also provides abundant resources to the Nuer, Dinka, and other peoples who have lived in the area for many generations. The continuing state of war in southern Sudan has forced the project to be abandoned, and it is unlikely to be completed in the near future.

Similar problems may arise in Ethiopia, where the Blue Nile and the Atbara rivers arise, providing 85% of Egypt's water. Egyptians are concerned about the possible future construction of dams for power supply or irrigation in the upper basins. Political instability in Ethiopia has made any large-scale hydro development impossible, but this situation may change in the future. There have been talks regarding the construction of a dam on Lake Tana, the source of the Blue Nile, and this may affect Egyptian control of Nile waters (Pearce 1991, p. 36).

A more real and pressing problem in the Ethiopian highlands is the widespread destruction of the forest or shrubby ecosystems in the upper basins. River regimes have become much more extreme, with extended droughts punctuated by periods of increased runoff. Intense erosion of the basin soils has caused a considerable increase in the solids content of the water and silting effects downstream. The Aswan Dam has been particularly affected by increased silting, which has reduced the length of its usefulness to merely a few decades.

The Aswan Dam in upper Egypt was completed in 1970; its inauguration allowed the opening for agriculture of extensive formerly arid lands. Apart from its initial positive impact on agricultural production, however, the dam has had a number of negative effects. One relates to conditions necessary for agriculture on the floodplain downstream from the dam. Because the dam has reduced the amount of silt reaching the plain, artificial fertilizers are required, increasing costs and affecting the water quality of the river. The newly irrigated soils have also been waterlogged, and salinization of soils and groundwater has become a common problem. Human health was affected by an increase in schistosomiasis. Construction industries suffered because they depended on a supply of alluvial silt to make bricks. Brick-makers often compete successfully with farmers for the same land. As a result, traditional farming areas have been reduced along with agricultural production.

The Nile basin is a fragile hydrographic system requiring careful management. Much coordination will be necessary to ensure that it is used appropriately and sustainably. However, management of such a complex and multinational basin is not merely a scientific endeavour. It encompasses political, social, economic, and historic issues. Only a holistic approach will permit resolution of its long-term problems without conflict and allow its optimum use to improve the quality of life of its population.

The Jordan River basin

Although the Jordan is a small river, it is located in an area where water resources are extremely scarce because of low precipitation (ranging from less than 100 millimetres in the south to about 500 millimetres in the northern highlands) and a history of acute political conflict between the countries sharing its basin (Lonergan and Brooks 1994).

There are five countries in the basin: Israel, Jordan, Lebanon, Palestine, and Syria. The upper basin is mainly in Lebanon and Syria, where the Hasbani and Banias rivers, together with other neighbouring springs in Israel, feed Lake Kinneret (the Sea of Galilee), which has a volume of 4 billion cubic metres. The main outlet from this lake is the Jordan River, whose waters are shared by Israel, Jordan, and the Palestinian West Bank. The total annual flow in the river brings 611 million cubic metres of water into the Dead Sea, whose salinity is 250 thousand ppm, or seven times that of seawater. To further complicate the political aspect, a considerable portion of the water flows underground (some toward the river valley and lakes and some toward the Mediterranean), increasing the chances for conflicts.

In an international basin such as this one, environmental management must be based on water-management policies and strategies. Every human activity depends in one way or another on the decisions that are made regarding water. Solving water issues in this part of the world will probably be the first step toward a lasting peace.

The Aral basin

For a long time, the Aral Sea in central Asia was the fourth largest lake in the world, with a unique ecosystem that had evolved in isolation for many millions of years and contained a diverse flora and fauna in its 50 thousand square kilometres.

During the early 1960s, the Soviet government implemented a mammoth irrigation project to grow cotton using water from the

Syr-Darya and Amudar'ya rivers. The project affected, directly or indirectly, the republics of Kazakhstan, Kirghizia, Turkmenistan, and Tajikistan. Unfortunately for the surrounding communities, the volume of the lake depended almost exclusively on water from these two rivers. Their flow was substantially reduced as water was diverted to cotton plantations. The amount returning to the rivers and the lake was, and still is, only a fraction of the previous volume and was heavily loaded with agrochemicals. After three decades, the Aral Sea is dying. Its ports are more than 80 kilometres from the lakeshore, its marshes and forests have perished, and the aquatic ecosystems have shrunk and lost much of their biodiversity (Pearce 1994a). The volume of water in the sea is only 40% of what is was only 33 years ago. Its volume continues to decrease by 27 cubic kilometres every year, the surrounding aquifers are drying up, and, in about 20 years, the sea is expected to disappear completely (Pearce 1994b).

The unsustainability of the model is clear. The cotton fields are waterlogged and the soil is becoming salty. There are almost no fish left in the lake. In some communities (such as Nukus), the water is unfit for drinking. Despite general agreement of the part of the various interested states that the situation must be improved, no targets or timetables have been set for doing so. In light of the current economic situation in the basin countries, it is doubtful that corrective measures will be implemented in the near future.

The Chad basin

The Chad basin is an endoreic hydrographic system extending over about 2.7 million square kilometres in the western part of central Africa. The northern portion of the basin lies in the semi-arid and arid regions of the Sahel and Sahara. The southern and eastern sections are mainly in the savannas of Sudan, Cameroon, and central Africa, although it occupies forested areas in the south. The basin is shared by several countries, of which the largest is Chad. It depends on the basin for most of its agricultural production and fisheries. The centre of the basin is occupied by a water-filled depression whose area varies with rainfall — Lake Chad.

The main rivers of the basin are the Chari and Logone, flowing from the highlands of Cameroon and the Central African Republic. These systems are, by far, the greatest suppliers of water to Lake Chad — 28 billion and 12 billion cubic metres per year respectively. These rivers flood their alluvial plains (the Yaeres) and the shores of the lake annually. The actual flooded area is estimated to be about 59 million hectares. The variations in the hydrological regime of the Logone River are important; at Baibo-Koum, a maximum flow of 4 438 cubic metres per second and a minimum flow of 13 cubic metres per second have been observed.

The Yaeres are the "breadbasket" of the Chadian region. Rice is cultivated using the floodwaters, and millet is planted in drier areas or after the floodwaters recede. Animal production is carried out in association with farming activities using itinerant strategies. Over 100 thousand animals are brought to the Yaeres annually to graze. Chadians also harvest an average of 80 thousand tonnes of fish annually from the basin.

In the 1960s, a large development project with international funding was proposed for the widespread irrigation of the Chad lowlands: the South Chad Irrigation Project. The project was to use the water to "green the surrounding deserts." Planning began in 1962, at the end of a period of unusually high rainfall. According to one designer, the project was a disaster. The hydrologic study was carried out over only 3 weeks, the idea of securing a different source of water "was dismissed out of hand," and it was assumed that the project was designed to operate for all water levels in the lake. In 1992, the intake areas were dry and many rotting ships were littering the landscape, often more than 60 kilometres from the lakeshore. As well, 4 thousand kilometres of canals were permanently dry and some villages that were flooded in 1962 were almost 100 kilometres from the shoreline.

This situation is not expected to improve over the medium or even long term. The lake loses 2 metres of water through evaporation every year and the flows of the Logone and Chari rivers have been cut in half. However, it is important to remember that in this case — as in many others — the problem does not lie in the natural variations of rainfall or in the high level of evaporation; rather, it lies in the manner in which the project was conceived, designed, and implemented and in the unnatural and nonparticipatory view of "development" that inspired the project from its inception.

The Colorado River basin

The Colorado River (Figure 2) rises in the Rocky Mountains and flows down the west face of Longs Peak, almost 4 thousand metres, as it begins its 2 400-kilometre journey to the Pacific Ocean. It receives runoff from the western areas of the Colorado, forming the Grand Valley where the first large irrigation developments are located. When the river enters this valley, its salinity is only 200 ppm; as it leaves the area after irrigating its crops, the salinity averages as much as 6 500 ppm.

Farther downstream, the river is joined by the Gunnison and the Green tributaries before forming the Powell reservoir behind the Glen Canyon Dam. Several new tributaries join the Colorado below this dam (Little Colorado and Virgin), increasing the flow, which is again dammed farther downstream forming several artificial lakes: Lake Mead above the Hoover Dam, Lake Mojave at the Davis Dam, and Lake Havasu at the Parker Dam.

The river then receives the brackish water of the Gila River, which increases its salinity slightly until it reaches one of the largest interbasin water-transfer operations in the world, the aqueduct to California, where one-third of its flow is pumped westward. The water is channeled into the Imperial Valley, Los Angeles, and San Diego to satisfy the needs of thousands of Californian farmers and millions of urban dwellers. Many of the fresh winter vegetables in the United States are produced using Colorado waters, and at least half of the water con-sumed in greater Los Angeles, San Diego, and Phoenix comes from the Colorado.

Only a small proportion of poor-quality water is left in the river when it finally crosses the Mexican border. To solve critical binational problems, a treaty was signed with Mexico in the 1970s to ensure bet-ter-quality water in the lower reaches of the river. Recently, the US

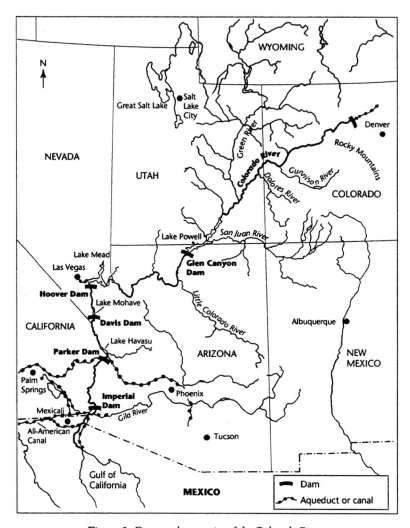

Figure 2. *Dams and reservoirs of the Colorado River.*

Congress approved investments in equipment for salt removal at a Yuma plant. It will cost $300 per unit to desalinate water that irrigators buy for $3.5 per unit upstream.

As will be described in Chapter 12, the Colorado River has been changed considerably, and not necessarily for good reasons. Today, the

6.
The Ogallala aquifer

The Ogallala aquifer is one of the largest and most heavily used ground-water reservoirs on Earth. Most of the water for irrigated farming in Texas, Kansas, Colorado, Oklahoma, New Mexico, and Nebraska comes from this huge underground basin. Continued overextraction has gradually reduced pressure in the aquifer — wells are no longer artesian, water levels have dropped, and pumping costs have increased. Lately, awareness of a vanishing resource has raised questions about the need to respect limits of renewability to protect the water resource.

Traditionally, sustainability of groundwater was not a concern in the US midwest. An example of the philosophy inspiring groundwater policy and decision-making in the field of resource management during the 1950s and 1960s (and today in some cases) is supplied by Felix Sparks, former head of the Colorado Water Conservation Board. When asked about the future of groundwater in the state, he responded with a rhetorical question: "What are you going to do with all that water? Leave it in the ground?" The state engineer in charge of water in New Mexico (Stephen Reynolds) further illustrated this line of thought: "We made a conscious decision to mine out our share of the Ogallala in a period of 25 to 40 years" (see Reisner 1986).

According to this approach, the solution to water scarcity was more water projects, including some that were very expensive and resulted in returns as low as 5% in economic benefits.

In Reno, Nevada, gambling and prostitution are legal, but for a long time water-metering was against the law.

river is largely an artificial system; aquatic life has been affected both in the river and in the Gulf of California; its flow has been curtailed; and its aquifers have been directly or indirectly modified, reducing the sustainability of the systems. The model of the Colorado River is another example of inadequate and nonparticipatory use of natural resources. We can only hope that the 21st century will see some of the worst effects of these pharaonic, 20th century hydroworks undone.

The aquifers of the western United States

Similar problems of widespread and thoughtless interference with nature can be observed in the aquifers and basins of central California. At the beginning of the century, almost all of California's water came from groundwater sources; now the proportion is 40%. The farmers of the central valley (Sacramento and San Joaquin valleys) overused the water and, by the 1930s, the farming economy was approaching collapse. The farmers convinced the legislature to authorize the Central Valley Project, by far the largest water project in the world; it was partially financed by the Roosevelt government. In the 1960s, the California Water Project, of similar size, was implemented. Together, these projects provide eight times the amount of water needed for the city of New York.

Despite the additional water, however, overuse continued because, instead of merely substituting the new sources for the older, overexploited sources, farmers opened up more land for cultivation. Estimates of the amount used over the renewal capacity of the aquifers in California range as high as 3 billion cubic metres per year, causing a growing water crisis throughout the state.

The lack of regulation pertaining to groundwater pumping, a traditional "absent" feature of the California legal system, has probably been a major factor contributing to the current critical situation (see box 6). However, cases of overexploitation of groundwater resources are not restricted to California or the United States. They can be found worldwide from the valley of Mexico to Bangkok, and from Manila to Havana.

8

$\mathcal{P}$rotecting $\mathcal{A}$ir $\mathcal{Q}$uality

The average person breathes about 12 cubic metres of air every day and dies if air supply stops for 5 minutes. The importance of air is obvious, and its monitoring and protection should be a top priority in any environmental program. Traditionally, in preindustrial societies, human activities did not have significant effects on air quality. In some cases, overcultivation or overgrazing could increase the local aerosol content. However, these effects could be considered minor when compared with the changes introduced in the atmosphere by the industrial revolution. Since the beginning of this technological revolution, many billion tonnes of fossil and nonfossil fuels have been burned. Today, several billion gallons of petroleum and tonnes of coal and other fuels are burned worldwide. The effects on air quality are felt almost everywhere. Changes are affecting practically all of its physical properties, including composition, concentration of particulates, temperature, and humidity.

Air and its principal contaminants

Normally, air at sea level contains about 78% nitrogen, 21% oxygen, and almost 1% argon. Carbon dioxide (CO_2) is present in smaller quantities (0.03%). The biologically active components of the atmosphere are CO_2 — the "raw material" for photosynthesis, which produces organic matter — and oxygen, which allows "burning" of this matter, forming CO_2 and completing the cycle.

In addition to the natural components of air, others, which appear in variable concentrations, are related to human activities. Some of these substances are considered "contaminants" because they may be harmful to human health. The main gaseous "contaminants" in air are sulphur dioxide, nitrogen oxides, carbon monoxide, chlorofluorocarbons, and ozone (Chovin and Roussel 1968).

Sulphur dioxide

Sulphur dioxide (SO_2) is produced naturally as a derivative of biological hydrogen sulphide (H_2S) and artificially by direct industrial emission (about 146 tonnes per year). It is highly soluble in water (10%); it combines with water to form sulphur trioxide (SO_3) and sulphuric acid (H_2SO_4), and with nitrogen to form ammonium sulphate ($(NH_4)_2SO_4$, which eventually falls in precipitation. Rain falling downwind of sulphur dioxide emissions can be very acidic (acid rain), affecting natural ecosystems, such as lakes or some forest soils.

Nitrogen oxides

Nitrous oxide (N_2O) is produced in small quantities by bacterial activity (about 600 million tonnes per year) and lightning. Artificial sources are important but, because this gas is not toxic, there is no need to alter them. Although nitric oxide (NO) is also produced naturally by bacterial activity (about 430 million tonnes per year), artificial sources are more important, particularly in combustion at temperatures above 1 300°C. It is removed from the air naturally by conversion to nitric acid (HNO_3) and nitrate salts, and in precipitation. It is very toxic.

Nitrogen dioxide (NO_2) is almost absent in nature. Its presence in the air is due to artificial processes, such as combustion at high temperatures (over 1 500°C). It is very toxic, and it is removed as nitric oxide.

Hydrocarbons

These substances (methane, ethane, ethylene, toluene, benzene, terpene, etc.) come from various natural sources, such as bacterial activity and leaks from gas fields. The main artificial hydrocarbon is terpene, which leaks from petroleum fields and refineries. About 20% of the hydrocarbons found in the air are artificial; of this amount, 75% comes from vehicles and 25% from industrial activities.

Carbon monoxide

Carbon monoxide (CO) is produced mainly from methane (CH_4) by chemical reaction with oxygen and hydroxyl ions (usually in swamps and other areas where methane is generated). Artificial sources relate to incomplete combustion processes (both in vehicle engines and industries). Carbon monoxide is very toxic to humans.

Carbon dioxide

This gas is produced by natural sources, such as cellular respiration, organic degradation, volcanoes, natural fires, natural dissolution of carbonates, etc. Artificial sources include artificial fires, industrial combustion, and combustion in vehicle engines. It is removed by photosynthesis, chemical and organic precipitation of carbonates, and burial of organic matter.

In strict terms, CO_2 cannot be considered a contaminant, but its excessive production by artificial sources without adequate removal can increase its concentration beyond natural limits, producing a "greenhouse effect" worldwide.

Chlorofluorocarbons

Chlorofluorocarbons (CFCs) are produced only artificially and are thought to reduce the density of stratospheric ozone molecules, increasing the effects of ultraviolet radiation. At ground level, the effect of CFCs is weak or nonexistent.

Ozone

Ozone is a natural component of the stratosphere. At ground level, however, its generation is related to various human activities, particularly automobile traffic.

Other contaminants

In addition to gaseous contaminants, many solid and liquid substances are often produced by industrial and engine emissions, traffic, or over-cultivation in dry soils and enter the air as aerosols.

Processes of contamination
in industrial and urban areas

Since its first stages of development, the industrial revolution caused episodes of acute air pollution in many cities. The air-quality problems in parts of Europe (London, the Ruhr basin, and the Moselle basin) during the last decades of the 19th century and first decades of the 20th century are well known. A similar situation developed in the northeastern United States (in Detroit, Pittsburgh, and New York), in Los Angeles, and in the largest industrial areas of Japan.

Eventually, in many cities, control measures (such as improved combustion and the use of filters) were implemented and noxious emissions were significantly reduced. Air pollution remains a problem, however, and most industrial zones in developed countries are also zones of poor air quality.

In Third World industrial and urban areas, air contamination became a problem later than in developed countries, but in cities like São Paulo, Mexico City, Santiago, Shanghai, Bangkok, Bombay, and Manila, conditions have been a "nightmare" for some time. Some Asian countries, such as China and India, owe this situation to their overdependence on coal. In other cases, air degradation is the combined result of the geographic concentration of high-emission industries and inadequate controls.

The case of São Paulo

São Paulo is located on the divide of the Serra do Mar about 60 kilometres from the Atlantic Ocean, at 650 to 1 200 metres above sea level. The dominant wind is from the southeast, with some influence of sea breezes because of the city's proximity to the ocean. The dispersion of air contaminants is slow during the winter as a result of frequent atmospheric inversions.

The worst contamination in the São Paulo region occurs in Cubatao, which is a valley 45 kilometres from the city on the Serra do Mar escarpment. The peaks of the Serra do Mar, which are a maximum of 1 000 metres above sea level, and the neighbouring Morrao and Quilombo hills enclose the basin, reducing air circulation. This area was selected as the site for many industries that were creating a critical situation in terms of air quality. At one time, Cubatao was one of the most contaminated areas of the world. Recently, an antipollution campaign has resulted in considerably lower levels of contaminants.

Because industrial sources are increasingly regulated, a higher proportion of current pollution can be blamed on vehicles.[8] In 1990, São Paulo contained about 3.5 million vehicles, of which 1.5 million were using gasoline; 1.5 million, alcohol; and 250 thousand, diesel fuel (CETESB 1992). Vehicles also produce most of the carbon monoxide, hydrocarbons, nitrogen oxides, and some sulphur oxides (Table 4). Industries are responsible for most of the aerosols and sulphur oxides. Diesel vehicles cause the most pollution, followed by gasoline-powered vehicles. Alcohol-burning engines appear to be relatively environmentally friendly. Because of an overconcentration of the population and an increasing number of vehicles moving at slower speeds in traffic jams, it is likely this situation will continue.

---

[8] However, the effect on the environment of widespread sugarcane plantations in previously forested areas and the poor management of refinery wastes cannot be overlooked.

Table 4. *Emission levels of pollutants ('000 tonnes per year) from vehicles and industry in metropolitan São Paulo.*

Source	CO	HC	NO$_x$	SO$_x$	MP
Vehicles					
Gasoline-powered	835	77.7	28.9	4.5	4.3
Alcohol-powered	172	14.3	10.0	—	—
Diesel-powered	218	35.6	159.0	73.0	9.9
Taxi	52	4.6	2.2	0.1	0.2
Motorcycle	32	6.1	0.2	0.3	0.1
Industry	39	12.0	14.0	44.0	44.0

Note: CO, carbon monoxide; HC, hydrocarbons; NO$_x$, nitrogen oxides; SO$_x$, sulphur oxides; MP, particulates.

Source: CETESB (1992).

The case of Los Angeles

For some time, metropolitan Los Angeles, the second largest urban area in the United States, has suffered from one of the worst cases of polluted air in the world. Its air violates federal health standards regarding levels of ozone, carbon monoxide, nitrogen dioxide, and fine particulates. The poor air quality is a direct result of a sustained increase in population, automobiles, and industrial activity. The population of the Los Angeles area tripled from 4.8 million in the 1950s to the current level of 14 million; at the same time, the number of vehicles increased by a factor of four from 2.3 million to 10.6 million. Some of the main sources of air pollution are motor vehicles, trash incinerators, barbecues, paints, dry cleaners, industrial coatings, and commercial ovens (Lents and Kelly 1993).

In 1947, heavy industries, foundries, motor vehicles, and backyard incinerators were identified as the sources of air pollution. The effects were most acute during periods of meteorological inversion, which are rather common on the Pacific coast of southern California. By 1953, Los Angeles' smog rivaled that of London.

To solve the problem, the Beckman Commission (chaired by Arnold O. Beckman of Beckman Instruments) was formed. It proposed five measures to decrease air contamination:

- Reduce hydrocarbon emissions;

- Set standards for automobile exhausts;

- Promote the use of trucks and buses that burn liquified petroleum gas instead of diesel fuels;

- Curtail the growth of the worst-polluting industries; and

- Ban the open burning of trash.

The recommendations of the commission developed into a general air-quality management plan for the region. An important step occurred when regional governments joined to form the South Coast Air Quality Management District (AQMD), with jurisdiction in Los Angeles, Orange County, Riverside, and part of San Bernardino. All American cities were to meet the standards set by the Federal Clean Air Act by 1987, although no one believed this would be possible for Los Angeles. Some of the measures that were implemented included:

- Banning of trash incinerators;

- Using vapour-recovery equipment to transfer petroleum products;

- Using nonreactive solvents[9] in industries using ozone-producing solvents (such as construction, auto manufacturing, and dry cleaning);

- Improving the quality of gasoline (by eliminating their lead content, for example);

- Installing devices in automobiles to prevent the emission of hydrocarbons; and

- Using catalytic converters.

As a result of these measures, any new car sold in California emits only 10% of the pollutants it emitted in 1970. In 1987, incentives were offered, to companies with more than 100 employees, to encourage carpooling and increase the number of people per car from 1.13 to 1.24. Despite these advances, the situation is still serious (Table 5). The main contributor is the motor vehicle (47% of hydrocarbons, 70% of nitrogen oxides, 90% of carbon monoxide, and 60% of sulphur oxides), followed

---

[9] Ironically, it was later discovered that these nonreactive solvents destroy the Earth's ozone layer.

Table 5. *Daily emission of pollutants in the Los Angeles area.*

Pollutant	Amount (tonnes)
Hydrocarbons	1 375
Nitrogen oxides	1 208
Carbon monoxide	4 987
Sulphur oxides	134
Particulates	1 075

Source: Lents and Kelly (1993).

by industries (26% of hydrocarbons, 18% of nitrogen oxides, and 30% of sulphur oxides).

According to the AQMD, the poor quality of the air is affecting the health of the population, increasing the annual costs of health-care systems by about $9.4 billion (Lents and Kelly 1993). About 15 million person-days are lost as a result of respiratory disease, and there is an increased risk of dying prematurely from exposure to particulates. According to this report, Los Angeles' failure to meet ozone standards is also costing 18 million person-days as a result of restricted activity, 65 million person-days from chest discomfort, 120 million person-days from coughing, 180 million person-days from sore throats, and 190 million person-days as a result of eye irritation.

Such data continue to prove that there is a basic problem that remains unsolved: the unsustainability of contemporary macrourban systems. Los Angeles is the perfect example.

The case of Mexico City

Mexico City is one of the most problematic areas in terms of atmospheric contamination. It is situated in a valley that is about 2 300 metres above sea level and, consequently, the content of available oxygen in the air is 23% lower than at sea level. The population of the valley is over 16 million, with approximately 2.5 million vehicles, and 30 thousand hydrocarbon-burning industries. The valley burns 43 million litres of hydrocarbons daily: 54% by vehicles, 28% by industries,

11% for domestic use, and 7% in thermoelectric plants. The high population density and intensive economic activity have gradually increased the amount of carbon monoxide, carbon dioxide, lead, sulphur, ozone, and nitrogen oxides in the air throughout the valley.

A large air-purification plan (Programa Integral contra la Contaminación Atmosférica en la Zona Metropolitana de la Cuidad México, PICCA), costing 4.7 billion dollars, has recently been launched. Its purpose is to reduce air pollution in the Mexican valley. Today, the trend of increasing air contamination has been stopped or even reversed. Improvements in the quality of fuels and adding catalytic converters to car engines under the program have had a positive effect. The air in the city is monitored automatically by 32 stations and manually at 19 stations. According to recent data, most atmospheric contaminants are below maximum allowable levels most of the time (except for ozone levels, which remain high).

Current and future trends

The seriousness of air-pollution problems and their effect on people's health have prompted policymakers and decision-makers in many urban and industrial areas to plan and implement campaigns to reduce the levels of contaminants produced by industries and vehicles. Although the results are clearly insufficient, some success has been achieved and the concentration of several contaminants has been significantly reduced. During the last few decades, there has been a reduction in the amount of coal burned, filters have been incorporated into chimneys, improvements have been made in combustion and other industrial processes, the use of solvents has been reduced, less trash is burned, and gasoline quality, car engine combustion, and exhaust systems have been improved to reduce harmful emissions.

The situation remains severe in many cities, however, especially in neighbourhoods and fragile ecosystems downwind of industrial areas. A persisting problem, for example, is the acid rain produced in the traditional industrial countries and some Third World areas, such as Brazil, China, and India, that still depend on coal. In most large cities, car emissions are still a concern that is often growing.

Recently, attempts have been made to improve coal-burning processes and, if successful, coal use will become less harmful, benefiting countries that still rely on it. Because coal is in plentiful supply, it is also possible that many countries that have abandoned it will begin using it again (Charles 1993).

9

Clean Energy for Planetary Survival

In preindustrial times, energy needs were limited to agrarian activities. Planting, harvesting, and transporting crops to small neighbouring urban centres did not require much energy. Transportation of merchandise and people was slow, and manufacturing (in foundries, potteries, and mills) was limited and consumed only small amounts of energy. Only minor quantities of energy were required to heat and light homes. These needs were satisfied by using animal, wind, and water power and by burning wood, charcoal, and other renewable fuels. Only negligible use of fossil fuels, such as coal, lignite, and peat, took place; and mining operations were limited to open-air quarries and pits.

Almost all preindustrial sources of energy were renewable. Forests could grow again naturally or be replanted, animals could be raised, wind and water were free. Under these circumstances, a steady rate of production and even some growth could be sustained for an unlimited period without exhausting the resource base. The effect on the environment of the use of these sources of energy was limited and, in most cases, only local. The impact of windmills and water mills was minimal, animal wastes contaminated only local areas and were biodegradable.

Before the industrial revolution, energy needs were satisfied through various renewable sources of energy, such as wind power (windmill in La Mancha, Spain).

The largest impact was probably a result of cutting trees for firewood: soil erosion and local decreases in biodiversity. At the global and regional levels, the effects were almost unnoticeable.

The industrial revolution

A dramatic change took place during the industrial revolution. Perhaps the most important element in the technological and social upheaval was the enormous increase in energy consumption. Industrial manufacturing required large amounts of energy to power the various types of engines that had been developed and spread throughout the rapidly expanding industrial world.

At the beginning of this period in Europe, energy needs were met by burning wood obtained from the many forests that covered the continent. Forests gradually disappeared from England, France, and

Germany, and rapid deterioration of the environment took place. Soils were eroded, gullies formed on the more vulnerable slopes, and catastrophic floods and alluvial sedimentation became commonplace (see Chapter 4).

Another, more powerful source of energy used from the beginning of the industrial revolution was coal. Large-scale coal mining began in the 18th century and expanded during the 19th century. Coal-producing areas, such as Wales and England, the Ruhr basin in Germany, the Moselle valley in France, and several areas in other European countries, became the main foci of industrial development.

The environmental impact of coal use was intense. Coal mining destroys the soil, and burning coal produces emissions of aerosols, sulphur compounds, and other associated pollutants. The widespread use of coal produced smog over the cities and acid rain downwind of coal-burning factories. Although the industrial revolution allowed phenomenal productive growth, it transformed the main industrial areas into environmental nightmares.

The use of hydroelectricity

Hydroelectric power was one answer to the increasing need for energy and the problems caused by burning wood and coal. Electricity had been discovered by the end of the 19th century and the spread of its use during the first decades of the 20th century allowed a new approach to energy production. The first large hydroelectric dams were built in the 1920s and 1930s. The Hoover Dam — constructed between 1930 and 1936 on the border between Arizona and Nevada, with a capacity of almost 1.4 million kilowatts and a volume of 3.36 million cubic metres — represented the largest single investment in energy production in history. Just 6 years later, the United States constructed a new dam, almost four and a half times more powerful with a capacity of almost 6.2 million kilowatts, at Grand Coulee, and this was only the beginning! The dam-construction spree spread quickly throughout the world. Thousands of dams were built in most industrial and in many nonindustrial countries and, in many cases, their distribution decisively influenced the location of industries and related urbanization.

Hydroelectricity has been considered to be one of the less risky sources of energy. Hydropower is renewable, it does not contaminate the environment, and it does not produce unwanted emissions. At most generating sites, however, there has been considerable environmental degradation:

- River ecosystems have been profoundly disturbed.
- Many biological species have decreased in number or disappeared.
- Large tracts of good land have been flooded.
- Extensive wetland ecosystems have been destroyed.
- Supplies of nutrients to downstream alluvial plains have decreased, harming farmers who depended on these natural fertilizers.
- Newly irrigated areas have become the focus of waterborne diseases.
- Soils have been salinized or have become waterlogged.
- Fishing communities have lost their livelihood.
- Indigenous peoples have been displaced from their traditional lands, with insufficient compensation often improperly awarded.
- Archeological sites have been covered by water.
- Hydrological regimes have been modified.
- Seismic activity has increased in some places.

The environment and societies may pay a high price for this "clean" energy. In some cases, the price can be too high.

The age of petroleum

The beginning of the 20th century also witnessed the gradual replacement of solid fossil fuels (coal, peat, and lignite) with liquid fuels (petroleum) and, later, gaseous fuels (natural gas) (see box 7). Until the first oil well was drilled — in 1859 in western Pennsylvania, reaching a depth of 21 metres — petroleum was used only marginally. A few decades later, a hundred wells were active throughout the United States and elsewhere.

The growing availability and use of fluid fuels facilitated the development of more standardized means of transportation. In the early 20th century, the invention of the automobile represented a quantum leap in the use of these fuels, which gradually became the main source of energy in industrial countries. By 1950, daily oil consumption reached 11 million barrels, growing to 46 million in 1970. In the 1970s and 1980s, continuing increases in oil consumption were somewhat curtailed by limited availability and higher prices. In the 1990s, however, daily petroleum consumption is high and still increasing.

The pattern of discovery and development of oil fields reveals that continuing increases in petroleum extraction will not be possible for more than a few decades. Even in the most optimistic scenarios, if growing consumption is not curbed, acute scarcity will be felt between 2030 and 2040.

The effects of petroleum exploitation and use are considerable. First, groundwater injected into geological formations to replace extracted oil depletes usable aquifers, some freshwater reservoirs become brackish, and oil spills contaminate other surface and subsurface geological formations.

Second, emissions from burning oil are often responsible for smog, for increased concentration of pollutant gases and aerosols, and for the increase in CO_2 levels in the atmosphere. Lately, more efficient

7.
Alcohol-powered cars in Brazil

In the 1970s, Brazil's energy strategy was based on the use of alcohol from sugarcane to power automobiles instead of gasoline. The experience was only partially successful. About half of the country's automobile fleet was converted to alcohol, but the early growth based on subsidies and support did not continue at the same rate when subsidies were discontinued. Currently, alcohol-fuel consumption is decreasing in Brazil, and nowhere else has alcohol been used for cars in a significant fashion.

The use of alcohol as fuel is not without problems. Although sugarcane is a renewable resource, its cultivation requires large areas of land, soil fertility is affected, erosion increases, and huge volumes of waste are produced. However, although the Brazilian government is abandoning open support for this alternative fuel, alcohol remains a major fuel for automobiles in Brazil.

oil-burning technology is reducing the amounts of obnoxious emissions; however, there will always be artificial emissions that contribute to the stress on the atmosphere.

Third, handling oil remains a hazardous enterprise. Currently, most petroleum is obtained offshore and transported by sea in large tankers. Accidents can produce environmental catastrophes in oceans, coastal areas, rivers, and lakes. Some oil spills from out-of-control wells may last for weeks and even months; in Kuwait, after the recent Gulf War, over 70 million tonnes of oil poured into the Persian Gulf. Tankers can break or sink, releasing huge volumes of crude oil. In the last 30 years, there have been more than 10 large oil spills in various coastal areas, several of which involved the release of more than 100 thousand tonnes of oil each into the sea: 300 thousand tonnes spilled as a result of the collision of the *Atlantic Empress* and the *Aegean Captain* off Trinidad and Tobago in 1979 (Funk & Wagnalls 1994); more than 200 thousand tonnes from the *Amoco Cádiz* on the coast of Brittany, France, in 1978; 250 thousand tonnes from the *Castillo de Beliver* in South Africa in 1983; and enough oil from the *Exxon Valdez* to contaminate 250 square kilometres of Alaskan coastal waters in 1989. As a result of these and other accidents and leakage, floating hydrocarbons have become a common feature of the world's oceans, affecting the flora and fauna.

Nuclear power

Nuclear power as a source of energy was developed in the 1950s and 1960s. The first nuclear power plant was built in 1954; by the end of the decade, there were six; 20 years later, there were several hundred. Nuclear energy became a pillar in the energy strategies of many developed countries. However, it took two accidents (Three Mile Island and Chernobyl) to raise widespread awareness of the risks and initiate a reassessment of the use of nuclear power. There is growing opposition from communities and municipalities to the installation of new nuclear power plants in their proximity. Few reactors have been built in recent years and the future role of nuclear power is in doubt.

The clean options

The increase in energy consumption during the 20th century has been rapid. Between 1900 and 1989, energy use grew from 21 to 318 exajoules.[10] Of this energy, about 88% comes from burning fossil fuels (Gibbons et al. 1989); the rest is obtained principally from nuclear and hydroelectric power. This distribution is the result of a general strategy based on fluid fuels, which was considerably shaken by the oil crisis of the early 1970s.

Today, well into the 1990s, the energy future of the planet is being looked at in a different light. Oil is becoming more difficult to find but, because it is easy to extract, transport, and use, it remains the main source of energy. Coal is easier to find, but "messy" to extract. In the long term, the main problem is that neither of these fuels is renewable and their volume is limited locally, regionally, and globally. In addition, their manipulation and use are environmentally "unfriendly" and risky.

Nuclear power is expensive and hazardous, as the problem of nuclear waste has not yet been solved. Hydropower has allowed growth of energy production in some areas, but has been identified as the cause of degradation of many river ecosystems, social dislocation of local communities, altered geological dynamics, and increased seismicity. The Brazilian alternative of alcohol from sugarcane is a renewable, easy-to-use energy source; however, its sustainability is doubtful.

A different approach altogether may be necessary. The world's "hard-path" supply policies are leading to a dead end. According to Bott et al. (1983):

> The desirable energy path is surely one of least risk (as distinct from least cost) for any given benefit...you will "never freeze in the dark" if you live in a super-insulated house and keep a few candles handy; you certainly run that risk if you live in a leaky house totally dependent on a distant nuclear power station.

---

[10] One exajoule is 10^{18} joules and is equivalent to the heat generated by burning 170 million barrels of crude oil.

It appears now that a different, softer strategy is possible. This new strategy can and must be based in large measure on renewable and cleaner sources of energy. Inexpensive solar energy can satisfy the energy needs of large numbers of homes and small industrial plants throughout the planet. Although insufficiently used, its potential is widely recognized. Wind energy is being harnessed locally, but its utilization could be expanded. Currently, a few wind farms represent an interesting attempt to explore the feasibility of using this energy source on a larger scale. There have also been attempts to tap the energy of tides, waves, and geothermal sources. There are many other potential clean sources of energy that could be further explored and developed (for a discussion of sustainable energy strategies, see Goldenberg et al. 1988). If new strategies consider these alternatives, it will be possible to reduce considerably the need for environmentally unfriendly energy resources.

One of the easiest ways to deal with the energy problem is to develop policies aimed at reducing consumption. In most countries, energy consumption is too high and wasteful, houses are not insulated, heating water takes much more energy that it should, urban transportation by cars instead of public transportation is inefficient, large volumes of water are released unused from some hydroelectric dams while other unnecessary hydroelectric projects are being built nearby, and pricing policies often promote wasteful behaviour rather than conservation.

Appropriate changes in technology and associated policies could radically alter the current situation: cars are becoming more economical, houses are better insulated, the use of solar energy is slowly increasing in some areas of the world, and pricing policies are being based on more conservationist principles.

Finally, there is growing awareness that energy cannot be isolated from the general model of societies. Social organization and energy strategies are two aspects of a whole. Development models must be sustainable, both in the short term and in the long term, and deal concurrently with socioeconomic and energy issues. A sustainable model must include not only energy production, adequate pricing policies, and well-conceived energy-producing systems, but also appropriate urban planning, sustainable basin management, and a holistic socioeconomic vision in the formulation and implementation of policies. Potential sources of clean energy are plentiful; if imagination and political will are applied systematically, there will be no reason to fear the future.

10

Africa in the 21st Century: Sunrise or Sunset?

With the end of the 20th century, sub-Saharan Africa is entering a new phase that is often viewed negatively. The 40-odd nations that are formally independent and recognized internationally display symptoms of disarticulation and impoverishment. The annual per-capita income in almost all countries of the continent is below $1 000 (Table 6). The $450 average annual income in the countries of the intertropical region puts this population in the lowest quarter in the world (WRI 1992). Some people have called this group of countries the "Fourth World."

During the last few decades, the participation of sub-Saharan Africa in international trade has fallen from 4% of world trade in the 1960s to 1.5% in the early 1990s, affecting its economic and geopolitical position. Today, many African nation-states are having trouble merely existing. There is little money to pay public employees, and national debts, which consume a large proportion of export revenues, are nearly impossible to service. In 1993, African debt stood at $140 billion. Some countries are paying more than a third of their export revenues in interest charges: Côte d'Ivoire, 41%; Ghana, 49%; Guinea-Bissau, 45%; Kenya, 33%; and Uganda, 81%. In most countries, income from legal exports does not cover the cost of the minimum

Table 6. *Per-capita income in sub-Saharan Africa.*

Country	Per-capita income (US$ per year)	Country	Per-capita income (US$ per year)
Angola	620	Liberia	450
Benin	380	Madagascar	230
Botswana	340	Malawi	180
Burkina Faso	310	Mali	260
Burundi	220	Mauritania	490
Cameroon	1 010	Mozambique	80
Cape Verde	780	Namibia	1 245
Central African Republic	390	Niger	290
Chad	190	Nigeria	250
Comoros	460	Rwanda	310
Congo	930	Senegal	650
Côte d'Ivoire	1 070	Sierra Leone	200
Djibouti	430	Somalia	170
Equatorial Guinea	120	Sudan	540
Ethiopia	270	Swaziland	900
Gabon	230	Tanzania	120
Gambia	380	Togo	390
Ghana	430	Uganda	250
Guinea	180	Zaire	260
Guinea-Bissau	790	Zambia	390
Kenya	380	Zimbabwe	640
Lesotho	470		

Source: WRI (1992).

amount of imported goods, and military expenses still absorb a large part of the states' budgets.

Many African governments have obtained assistance from richer countries in the form of "soft" loans, subsidies, technical support, and, to a much lesser degree, preferential commercial treatment. This has encouraged them to become dependent on international aid to the extent that, if this assistance decreased, their political equilibrium would be disrupted and their institutional structures would be threatened. In some cases, official development assistance (ODA) accounts for a large part of the countries' gross national product (GNP). ODA amounts to 74.2% of Mozambique's GNP; in Guinea-Bissau, 64.4%; in the Gambia, 50.7%; in Somalia, 47.6%; in Cape Verde, 32.2%; in Tanzania, 31.8%; and in Equatorial Guinea, 30.4%.

The causes of poverty

There is widespread belief that some of the more critical problems experienced by African countries are related to the frequent natural catastrophies (mainly droughts) and wars. In some cases, there is an element of truth to this interpretation, but in many others the issues are much more complex, and the causes must be found elsewhere.

The notions of drought and aridity are only partially related to meteorological data. In the "arid" countries, such as those of the Sahara and Kalahari regions, drought is an elusive concept. Arid climates are dry by definition, and in most cases irregularity of rainfall is normal. Therefore, years of little rain cannot be called "drought" years; dry years are part of predictable climatic patterns to which pastoral and oasis societies have adapted for a long time. If no external factors are introduced, traditional production and social systems tend to survive these "drier" periods without major problems.

In semi-arid countries where pastoral activities are combined with planting of rain-fed crops, the occurrence of arid spells has been traditionally mitigated by trade with more humid neighbouring regions. When dry periods extended beyond a certain period, conflicts arose, but this was more the exception than the rule. In brief, drought is not the root cause of African poverty and other problems, it only exacerbates them.

Wars present a different problem. They have become all too frequent in Africa. In most cases, they are a main cause of some of the more desperate situations. They can bring economic activities to a halt: production systems are reduced, distribution of goods is disrupted, and social systems can be seriously damaged or even destroyed. Nevertheless, wars are a consequence of the African situation, not its basic cause.

From an economic point of view, the main apparent reason for African "underdevelopment" is its low levels of production, measured in terms of both gross domestic product (GDP) and exports. In fact, with few exceptions, exports and GDPs of African countries have been decreasing consistently over the last few decades. This has been coupled with sustained and widespread demographic growth. When GDP decreases and population increases, per-capita income shrinks, reducing the availability of financial resources for both the state and the population.

A second element in this "image of poverty" relates to the gradual fall of international trade figures for the continent. The decrease in exports appears to be a result of a complex array of factors. One such factor is the decline in the terms of exchange for traditional African products, such as cocoa, copra, cotton, and palm kernels. Between 1977 and 1989, cocoa prices fell from $5.41 to $0.94 per kilogram; copra from $574.7 to $264.7 per tonne; cotton from $2.22 to $1.27 per kilogram; and palm kernels from $466 to $190.9 per tonne. Another factor is the disappearance of markets for these products, frequently because of changes in consumption trends. On the other hand, it is also a by-product of a widespread loss of competitiveness, mainly because of the dislocation of national production or commercialization systems, and of inadequate use of natural resources.

Population growth

Persistent increases in the population exacerbate the other factors. In most African countries, population growth is over 2% annually; in some, it reaches 3.5% or more; for example, Côte d'Ivoire, 3.78%; Kenya, 3.58%; Uganda, 3.67%; and Zambia, 3.75%. The overall average for Africa is 2.98%, higher than any other continent. This is due to continuing high birthrates and decreasing death rates.[11]

Population pressure has been one of the main forces promoting the various environmental degradation processes. Overgrazing, overcultivation, excessive or inappropriate use of water resources, deforestation, and elimination of natural ecosystems are, among other reasons, a direct

---

[11] Recently, death rates have begun to increase again, mainly because of wars and the AIDS epidemic. Deterioration of the health-care system is also having an effect.

result of overpopulation for existing forms of production and land-occupation systems.

Political upheaval

Sub-Saharan Africa seems to be engaged in a continuing series of conflicts between national and tribal groups. This political instability weakens the economies of the countries, affects the production-planning process and is an important factor in preventing populations from overcoming their difficult situation.

In the mid-1990s, open conflicts are continuing, having just started or recently ended in Angola, Chad, Ethiopia, Liberia, Mozambique, Sierra Leone, Somalia, and Sudan. The recent conflict in Rwanda is a tragic part of this trend. This continuous state of war has made the economic crisis more acute, disrupting production, marketing, and distribution systems and leading to famine, high mortality rates, and other social hardships. To better understand the root causes of the African situation, however, we must go back in history to the early beginnings of humankind.

Historical causes of the current situation

The origin of humankind

Africa is the place of origin and centre of dispersion of the human race. For this reason, its ethnic diversity is the richest on the planet. From the peoples of Hamitic roots of the Sahara and Sahel to the Bantu groups of the more humid regions of the forest periphery, and from the Pygmies of the tropical rain forests to the Bushmen of the southern deserts and steppes, the continent possesses the largest variety of clearly differentiated human groups.

African agricultural societies developed with the domestication of cereal crops, such as sorghum and millet, and grazing animals (bovines, sheep, goats, and, finally, camels), which allowed the establishment of more sedentary communities in the savannas and associated forests. This process probably began in the Nile, Sudanese, and Sahelian savannas, and spread south and east. At least part of the African savanna is of secondary origin, developing after the anthropogenic destruction of intertropical forests (mainly through burning) as they were cleared for crop and animal production a few thousand years ago.

The oldest focus of agricultural development was in the valleys of the Nile and its tributaries. The main areas settled were the Nile delta, the lower part of the Egyptian fluvial plains, the middle and upper Nile, the northern zone of present-day Sudan (Nubia), the southern plains of the White Nile (which flows northward from the Ugandan highlands), and the sedimentary plains of the Blue Nile and Atbara rivers, both of which descend from the Ethiopian plateau. This culture was based on the domestication of cereals, such as wheat; controlling periodic flooding of the Nile alluvial plain; and domestication of ruminants, such as *Bovis primigenius*. The agrarian culture extended south along the main rivers to present-day Sudan and finally to Ethiopia, where it remained isolated and relatively unchanged for a long time.

Agricultural development and the need for water management promoted the evolution of state-type political structures in Egypt, based on a theocratic and absolutist regime and ideology: the time of the pharaohs. The political and ideological influence of this culture extended southward, as did its agrarian aspects. The example of these agricultural states was replicated first toward Ethiopia and Sudan and later westward along the Sudanese belt to the Atlantic coast. The political empires of Ghana and Mali, the Hausa and Songhai kingdoms, were based in large measure on this agrarian economy as well as the political elements that went with it.

The Sudanese people were probably the first to domesticate cattle in sub-Saharan Africa (a practice apparently adopted from the Mediterranean region via Egypt and the Nile valley), and the Nilotic or Bantu people were perhaps the first to grow some varieties of sorghum and millet. With time, some groups (mainly Bantu) moved southeast, settling in the east African savannas (in what is now Kenya, Mozambique, Tanzania, and Zimbabwe), where agrarian states developed, such as the "Zimbabwe" civilization near Harare. When European settlers arrived in South Africa, a process of gradual encroachment of migrating agropastoral Bantu-speaking groups (the Tswana, Sotho, Basuto, Zulu, and Swazi) was taking place, simultaneously displacing or assimilating the Khoisan autochthonous groups (Hottentots and Bushmen).

Another important aspect of sub-Saharan evolution was the development of trans-Saharan trade, both along the Atlantic coastal routes and through the desert. In large measure, the prosperity of Carthage in Roman times was due to its control of the trans-Saharan trade routes, through which it received ivory, gold, and slaves. Later, after the Mohammedan expansion of the 8th century to the Maghreb, the Moorish and Moroccan empires also based their power on controlling these trade routes into the heart of Africa. The development of the Sudanese and Sahelian kingdoms was greatly facilitated by the concentration of resources that resulted from this trade. Some of the Sahelian cities (such as Timbuktu) developed and thrived as a result of this commercial activity; important episodes of southward political expansion (particularly Moroccan) brought lasting effects of Islam to the Sudan and the Sahel.

A parallel spread of Islam was taking place on the eastern coast, particularly because of the Arab–Omani and the Malay influence and the growth of sea trade in the Indian Ocean.[12] As a result, several Afro-Arabian cities developed: Zanzibar, Dar es Salaam, Pemba, Mombasa, etc.

The rain forests remained unsettled for some time to come, until forest-adapted domestic plant species appeared on the African scene. The white yam (*Dioscorea rotundata*) and the yellow yam (*Dioscorea cayenensis*) were domesticated in West Africa. Other crops were introduced from Asia — old cocoyam (*Colocasia* sp.) and the water yam (*Dioscorea alata*) — and later from America — new cocoyam (*Xanthosoma* sp.) and cassavas (Hahn and Ker 1980, p. 5).

Raising domesticated animals in a forest environment was limited because of the effect of the tsetse fly and other lethal diseases on cattle and other large mammals (including humans). Later, first through

---

[12] The Malay were expert seafarers and reached Africa about 1 800 years ago, settling in Madagascar and other coastal areas of eastern Africa.

deforestation and later through efforts directed at insect pests, more extensive occupation of the forest was possible.

Some of the more ancient groups, like the Pygmies, were the first to move into the forest. They developed an extractive and itinerant farming culture adapted to the complex jungle environment. These groups developed well-adjusted, sustainable production systems that permitted their survival in the hostile jungle environment with only minor changes for many thousands of years.

For the Bantu-speaking (and other) farming people, the process of occupation took place in a different manner. These groups were essentially savanna dwellers. Unlike the Pygmies, who settled the forest from the inside, this group approached from the periphery. Areas were cleared for farming and used for only a few years because of the limited fertility of forest soils. Subsequently, the farmers would move to a different site and continue the cycle.

With time, these peoples, with their two types of production systems, spread throughout the rain-forest region: the itinerant farmers at the periphery and in clearings and the "forest people" more symbiotically adapted to the natural ecosystem. For many centuries, this dual and combined approach to occupation and exploitation of the forest environment developed and stabilized.

In forested regions, communication by land was difficult because of the dense vegetation. Therefore, agricultural expansion occurred mainly along fluvial paths, with small islands of human occupation. The agroforestry societies formed by this process were isolated; their political units were very small and their cultural diversity was great.

Africa in the 15th century

In the mid-15th century, when Portuguese explorers arrived in Africa, they found a savanna region containing small and medium-sized kingdoms based on combined agropastoral production systems and a commercial framework structured along the trans-Saharan routes in the west, through the Nile valley in the northeast, and along the Indian Ocean routes in the east.

These kingdoms were usually quite small, with populations of no more than 30 or 40 thousand. They often remained within ethnically defined borders, separating people of different cultures, ways of life, languages, dialects, and religions. Their political organization was stable, but their political configuration was not. In forest regions, local groups developed in relative isolation and the resulting kingdoms were very small, normally with several hundred or thousand people and covering a few hundred square kilometres or less.

In any case, African political units were based on geographic locale, a common agropastoral economic base, a particular situation in relation to commercial fluxes, and, overall, common traditions, language, religion, and culture. Occasionally, some groups dominated others or groups might merge or divide. In general, however, they tended to stabilize according to national or ethnic identities. In these political units, government structures were relatively small: a ruling group or family with a small number of officials. The ruling group or "class" was often determined by production surpluses in the particular society.

Cities developed at the points of convergence of the trade routes — Dongola in the Upper Nile, Timbuktu on the Niger, Mombasa and Dar es Salaam on the Indian Ocean — giving rise to more powerful political entities, with a larger concentration of population and resources, and well-defined bureaucracies. In most cases, these cities controlled small territories and acted as commercial-exchange centres.

The arrival of Europeans

European explorers, traders, and military forces arrived mainly by sea, although, later, they penetrated the interior on foot, on horseback, or by boat along the few navigable rivers. In the first phase, their arrival promoted the development of several coastal ports. New commercial centres, particularly slave-trading harbours, arose on the coast of Guinea (displacing the Sahelian trade oases) and in the ports of eastern Africa. In the latter phase, European forces gradually overpowered the Swahili and Arab elites, taking control of the whole coastal zone.

The expansion of trade, together with colonization and deforestation of coastal areas and the secondary savannas of the hinterland,

strengthened several African states — the Ashanti and Yoruba kingdoms in the current territories of Ghana and Nigeria respectively.

Later, in the 19th century, when European powers consolidated
their control, they expanded toward the interior until a new political
distribution took place. This process of European colonization, which in
principle was based on slave trade, became reoriented toward the
exploitation of natural resources for export to Europe using slave or
semi-slave labour. Copper mines were opened in British Northern
Rhodesia (now Zambia), gold mines and placers were established in
Southern Rhodesia (now Zimbabwe), and banana, cocoa, copra, and
many other indigenous and introduced crops were grown throughout
other suitable areas. Gradually, the slave ports became exporting centres
for local production.

Colonial territorial boundaries were decided by political agreements in Europe with no consideration of existing ethnic, linguistic,
cultural, and religious boundaries. Almost all European colonies in
Africa included people from various African nations, and many nations
were divided by artificial borders.

Often, the new administrative systems ignored traditional organizations, imposing "unnatural" units on the local peoples in an authoritarian and arbitrary manner. In other cases, mainly in British areas,
traditional structures were adapted for colonial administration.

Inheriting irrational borders and colonial structure

When African independence movements succeeded, the newly formed
states had to deal with the artificial boundaries established by the
Europeans. In some cases, such as the Belgian Congo (now Zaire) and
Tanganyika (now continental Tanzania), the new states were very
large; in others, like the Gambia and Equatorial Guinea, they were
small or had odd configurations.

These nations are paying a price for these artificial arrangements,
which ignored traditional organizations and knowledge. In many countries, the commercial crop-exporting systems have deteriorated, and
financial resources are insufficient to maintain state bureaucracies, para-
lyzing administrative functions. In addition, the commercially oriented

rural productive system is increasingly unable to keep up production levels and provide enough jobs; the result is massive rural migration to the cities.

The problem is not helped by the gradual decrease in farming surpluses, necessary to feed the cities. In some countries, even the farmers are having difficulties feeding themselves. Another important cause of the overconcentration of people in cities is the migration and resettlement of "refugees of war" (such as in Angola, Mozambique, and Somalia). Unfortunately, there are neither jobs nor services for the millions moving to urban areas, and conflicts between the various nations or tribes are becoming more frequent, pushing many African societies into a chronic crisis situation.

Wars are environmentally unfriendly

The case of Angola

Angola is a large country with important mineral resources (such as petroleum and diamonds), great biodiversity in forests and savanna ecosystems, extensive areas suitable for agriculture and rangelands, and important fisheries. Because it is not densely populated — about 10 million people in 1 million square kilometres — the resource base would be more than enough to provide a high quality of life to the population.

However, a large portion of Angola's productive base has been degraded or eliminated. Forests have been burned or logged; many wildlife species have disappeared; roads, railroads, airports, and buildings have been rendered useless; and people have emigrated, making Angola a country of refugees. All of this is the result of war.

The Movimento para a Liberação do Angola (MPLA), a leftist nationalist movement, was founded by an Angolan intellectual and poet (Agostinho Neto) in 1956 to fight for Angola's independence from Portugal. Some years later, the Frente Nacional para a Liberação do Angola (FNLA) was founded by Holden Roberto, an Angolan militant, and an offshoot, UNITAS, was established in 1966 by Jonas Savimbi.

In 1975, when the country finally won its independence, there were disagreements between the Soviet-supported MPLA and the other two movements (FNLA and UNITAS), which were supported by the United States and South Africa. War broke out. Within the framework of the Cold War, several countries from both blocs were involved directly or indirectly (Cuba, the former Soviet Union, South Africa, and the United States). Many years later, although the Cold War has ended, the conflict in Angola persists.

The reason for the persistence of the war probably relates to deeply ingrained ethnic feelings that were poorly managed during Portuguese colonial times. There is a dichotomy within Angolan society, as in other African countries: a "Europeanized" elite, which is politically left of centre, and a traditionally based movement, UNITAS, which is rightist. One reason for the apparent success of UNITAS is probably related to its support from the numerous Ovimbundu; support for the Luanda government is mainly based on the mixed-culture urban population.

The European models and ideologies fail to address local problems and, as a result, a populist movement can grow using whatever support is available (even a racist regime, as in South Africa in the late 1970s and early 1980s). After 30 years of fighting, the Angolan war is still going on, producing widespread social and material degradation.

One of the victims of the conflict is the environment: forests have been burned, animals have been hunted in an indiscriminate way, and mines and other explosive devices have been buried in many areas. The productive base is rapidly shrinking. The formal Angolan state is gradually falling apart. This is probably more than an ethnic war, however. In our interpretation, we are witnessing the end of a model alien to the true Africa. Soon, gradually and painfully, a new society, more informal and based on tradition, will probably arise from the ruins of colonial and neocolonial Angola.

The case of Nigeria

Nigeria is another country in which an inherited political system and boundaries have caused problems, and where both society and the environment are suffering the consequences. The British colony in Nigeria included in the same political unit several ethnic groups with a history of conflicts and rivalries: the Yorubas, the Ibos, and the Hausas.

As soon as independence was declared in 1960, a bloody war (the Biafra war) erupted between the Yoruba and Hausa dominated government and the Ibo population of the southeast. The war ended in 1962 with the defeat of the Ibos, and for some time it seemed that Nigeria would become a viable political entity. It was the most populated African nation, with 75 million people, one of the world's largest producers of petroleum, and one of the richest countries on the continent.

During its three and a half decades of independence, however, several military governments with no accountability held power, while misappropriation of funds and bribery were the rule. Today, Nigeria has a population over 100 million, unemployment is widespread, crime is rampant, public utilities seldom work, and consumer goods, and even fuel, are hard to find. In brief, the whole administrative structure is barely functioning and the formal economy is disintegrating.

The political system is not working well either. After 8 years of authoritarian regimes, elections were held in June 1993. However, President Babamgida refused to relinquish power when Moshood Abiola, a nonmilitary Yoruba candidate chosen by him, was elected. By mid-1994, Mr Abiola had been arrested and the country was in extreme turmoil, with the southern Yoruba region threatening to separate and the government trying to enlist the southeastern Ibos as allies (until now, unsuccessfully; see *Economist* 1994c). The traditional Nigerian nations — Hausas, Yorubas, and Ibos — and several other national groups are now locked inside artificially drawn borders and there is constant political and ethnic tension. Even if this crisis is solved, it is likely that another will soon emerge. The problem does not seem to lie with the political leaders, but rather with the whole political system, including inappropriate territorial boundaries.

Nigeria's environment has also suffered the consequences of the economic crisis. The rapid population growth, particularly in and around the largest cities (Lagos and Ibadan), has affected natural ecosystems. Formerly a forested country, Nigeria has lost most of its forest ecosystems. Wildlife has disappeared, rivers and coastal waters are increasingly contaminated, soil erosion (which was practically unknown before) has become one of the main problems affecting agriculture, and industrial development has been paralyzed because of problems with the supply of basic inputs, such as fuel, water, and electricity.

As in Angola, however, Nigeria's future may lie in the gradual growth of a new, more African approach to social and environmental management (*Time* 1993). Former foreign minister, Joseph Garba, said, "Nigeria will go back to the Stone Age." It will not be a stone age, but rather a more traditional age, still modern, but based on African roots.

Evolution of environmental management in Africa

Africa's history has produced effects on the environment that cannot be found in other areas of the world. As the cradle of humanity, ecosystems adapted to human presence and human technologies as they evolved. This is probably one of the reasons why such a wide array of large mammals is found in Africa, compared with other continents, which were occupied by humans at a later stage.

Preagricultural human occupation had effects on the environment. Hunter–gatherers and fishing cultures overhunted some species, over-collected or artificially dispersed seeds, and burned forests, bush, and herbaceous ecosystems for hunting or other purposes, deliberately or accidentally modifying the environment.

Farming and the domestication of animals introduced additional changes. Some species (cattle, goats, sheep, camels, etc.) were tamed for their meat, milk, leather, and other by-products; some were tamed as helpers or companions (cats and dogs).

Agriculture required the clearing of land for cultivation. After growing several crops and depleting the soils, the fields were abandoned and new ones opened. In many cases, after many "slash-and-burn" cycles, the original forest ecosystem was converted to secondary savanna, made up of a herbaceous cover and few bushes and trees (Figure 3).

Gradually, savanna ecosystems and associated cultures reached a sort of equilibrium; grassy areas with low soil fertility were used for

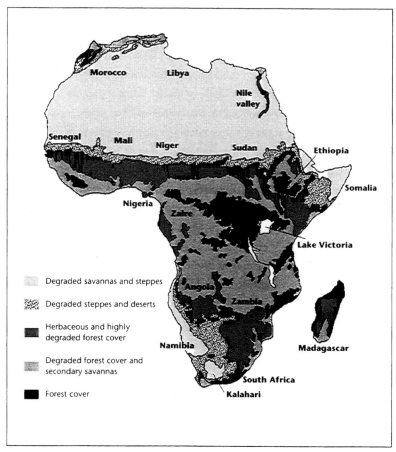

Figure 3. The ecozones of Africa.

grazing and the best soils were used for farming. In these savanna environments, two different cultures developed in close association, almost
of a symbiotic nature: nomadic shepherds, such as the present-day
Fulani and Peul in the Sudan and Sahel and the Masai in eastern
Africa, and sedentary farmers, such as the Bambara in Mali.

There are more humid forest areas that remained untouched,
mainly because of the lack of crop species adapted to this type of environment and the presence of deadly diseases, such as sleeping sickness.
The first forest dwellers, such as the Pygmies of the Congo region, based

their survival on hunting, fishing, and gathering; farming was only a secondary activity. They were (and still are) nomadic and became very well adapted to the forest environment. With the development of appropriate crop species, more sedentary cultures began to encroach on forest areas. The approach of both of these cultural groups tended to preserve most of the original components of the forest ecosystem. Although there was some impact, mainly through selective gathering or overgathering, or artificial spreading of some species and varieties, the forest structure remained unchanged, with several tree strata, dense undergrowth, rich genetic diversity, and its strong effect on hydro-dynamics, preventing runoff and soil erosion.

European settlers promoted or imposed the development of planta-tions, which gradually encroached on many forested areas. As a result, forests receded to a fraction of their former area. This progress was increased when pest control, antibiotics, and vaccines were developed to overcome the disease hazard. Now, forested areas in Africa cover less than 20% of their former area and soil erosion is widespread.

A different problem occurred in semi-arid and arid lands where rain-fed agriculture was impossible without some form of irrigation. By and large, steppe and desert cultures were based on the herding of sheep, goats, and camels. The potential for environmental degradation by these peri-desertic groups was limited to the proximity of water holes, which were few and often far apart. Sheep and goats require water almost daily, and camels once a week; therefore, herds could not be driven much beyond 2 to 4 days' travel to the next water holes or places where water containers could be stored. As a result, most of the steppe and the savanna ecosystems remained relatively untouched. Natural springs are rare in semi-arid and arid areas; therefore, most water holes were hand-excavated in wadi (arid "river" valleys) or plains in alluvial or related eolian sediments. Wells were dug wherever the depth to good-quality water was less than 30 to 40 metres.

Several technological developments changed this situation. First, new hydrogeologic techniques, such as drilling and geophysical logging allowed identification and exploitation of much deeper and sometimes better-quality, higher yielding aquifers. Second, the development of new types of mechanical pumps permitted larger volumes of ground-water to be extracted over shorter periods. Finally, the spread of motor vehicles made possible the transportation of water from wells to drier areas. As a result of these developments and the influence of a culture that based prestige on possession of the largest number of animals, herds and herders rapidly increased.

These were the main causes of increased desertification in the Sahelian and peri-Saharan regions. Widespread overgrazing took place and, in a few decades, the southern boundary of the Sahara advanced southward by tens or even hundreds of kilometres. As a result of the new water resources, the density of people and livestock increased considerably (from 5 to 15 people per square kilometre). In 1985, over-stocking had been estimated at 22% in the Sudan (Pearce et al. 1990) and similar figures seem to be common in all the cattle-raising areas of the Sudanese and Sahelian regions. Even during rainy years, the vegetation near the wells was heavily damaged. When the drought of 1973–1975 struck, the cattle ate everything. Even trees were stripped of their branches, and thousands of animals died. Because of the drought, the plants did not regenerate and an acute famine followed. A well-meant "development assistance" program, which had not considered all aspects of the problem, introduced a technical element that inappropriately changed traditional cultural and production patterns that were well adapted to the local environment.

The development of large cities throughout the steppe, savanna, and forested regions and the rising price of fuel have caused an increase in the amount of wood cut for use as fuel for cooking, industrial ovens, and other purposes. The final result of this has been the retreat of forests farther and farther away from urbanized areas. This process can be observed throughout the continent; even in oil-producing countries, wood is widely used for domestic and other purposes. In 1983, it was estimated that, at 43 million cubic metres, the annual consumption of fuelwood and charcoal in the Sudan represented more than 90% of the total production of wood country-wide (Pearce et al. 1990). Similar figures are reported from Mali, Niger, and other countries in the Sudanese and Sahelian regions.

Another cause of environmental degradation in Africa relates to the construction of poorly designed hydro projects, especially irrigation and storage systems and hydroelectric dams. One of the prime examples of failure was the Lake Chad irrigation system built in the 1970s (see Chapter 7). This project was planned without considering the climatological regime, which is characterized by regular cycles of drought and flood. The many millions of dollars spent on the project have resulted in the construction of kilometres of useless channels that, for most of the time, remain dry. Often the negative impact of such projects could have been predicted if an independent, in-depth study had been conducted beforehand.

There are several projects in the planning stage that may entail similar or even larger risks: the Jonglei canal in the Sudd wetlands of southern Sudan; and the trans-basin transfer of water from the Congo River to the Chad basin through the Chari and several other rivers. A lack of funds, continued political instability, and a growing sense of the risks of these megaprojects have slowed the actual execution of these projects. New endeavours will probably require in-depth impact assessments, hopefully reducing the risks of repeated failures in the future.

Old and new development models

The complex situation in present-day Africa is the result of a long history of outside interference and ongoing internal processes. The main problem, with negative implications for the future, is deterioration of the resource base, which may be irreversible: deforestation, destruction of ecosystems, depletion and contamination of water resources, loss of fertility and erosion of soils, and widespread habitat destruction may be permanent. A major consequence of these processes is a decrease in production in many rural areas. The volume of exports is lower; therefore, less foreign currency is entering the countries. Coupled with the need to service the continent's $140 billion debt, these factors are increasing the difficulty of acquiring many basic imports.

As a consequence of changing many farming areas from subsistence to commercial production and decreased production, rural migration rates are high, producing continuous, unsustainable demographic growth of cities throughout the continent.

In some countries, there is a trend toward consolidation of the strongest national groups, providing the minimum political stability necessary for defining new, sustainable developmental alternatives. In other countries, with two or more national groups competing for power, political instability may increase. In some cases, the trend toward political fragmentation may succeed. It is possible that there will also be realignments beyond the inherited "colonial" borders. Generally, the trend seems to be one of progressive substitution of the "colonial-type" state, with its formal institutions and economy poorly adapted to African conditions, by a system that is based more on traditional institutions and the informal sector.

In the more densely populated areas, acceleration of urbanization processes appears to be taking place, with development of a new "Afro-urban" culture that may gradually allow the sowing of the seeds of a new institutionalization. The tendency also seems to be toward a renationalization of states with redefined borders and institutions. This process is taking place mainly as a result of a succession of conflicts, which may persist for several decades with continuous effects of disarticulating production systems, affecting the quality of life of the populations of many countries for some time to come. If this trend continues, famines may develop and mortality rates may increase again (although perhaps in a localized manner in relation to armed conflicts or epidemics such as AIDS). This is likely to occur simultaneously with a continued decrease in birthrates, which, coupled with migration, may tend to stabilize the population levels in the medium or longer term. It can also be expected that, as in Latin America and some Asian countries, the growth of African cities may slow as they become less and less attractive places to live because of social and environmental degradation.

The failure of the "colonial," "socialist," and "capitalist productivist" models will promote the search for new models based on African indigenous resources and cultures. Gradually, we expect that a revaluation of the role of the agricultural village and the communal grazing system will take place, together with a trend toward political

*The divergence between the green revolution model and local traditional cultures
is a serious obstacle to sustainable development in Africa
(irrigated farm near Dongola, Sudan).*

decentralization as a result of a predictable shrinking of the central power. The new indigenous-based models may allow management approaches combining traditional systems with scientific know-how.

Generally, the renationalization process may begin with greater dependence on foreign aid, which may later decrease because of a "drying up" of funds or "aid fatigue" in developed countries. At a still later stage, the deterioration of state economies resulting from the decreasing resource base and disarticulation of the formal production systems may promote forces of self-management and self-development in a framework of growing decentralization. They may even include reruralization processes.

Outside interference has proved to be the cause of much unhappiness for African society. A successful, sustainable, and equitable model, respectful of Africa's diversities and resources, will only be developed through the indigenous growth of authentic, locally inspired solutions. This process will be difficult and painful, but it is essential if Africa is finally to define its future in its own terms.

11

Latin America and the Caribbean: A History of Environmental Degradation

Environmental changes in Latin America and the Caribbean during the last few centuries are probably unparalleled in other parts of the world. During this period, the continent has experienced widespread and increasingly dense human occupation of formerly sparsely populated areas and a general process of urbanization that catapulted provincial-sized cities into huge megalopolises of many millions.

As a result of these changes, most indigenous ecosystems were profoundly transformed: forests became savannas and farmlands; grasslands became crops or forests; deserts were irrigated; aquifers were depleted; rivers, lakes, and coastal waters were contaminated; biodiversity has been under constant attack; and quality of life has deteriorated or is under threat. Thus, one of the richest continents in natural and cultural diversities, with the strongest resource base, has been losing all of it at an alarming rate. The most serious concern is that the process is not slowing; on the contrary, it seems to be accelerating daily.

What caused this situation? Where are the problems most acute? What are the effects of globalization? What can be done to prevent further degradation? The answers to these questions are not simple or

straightforward; they are the result of a peculiar historical evolution and
a unique natural geography.

Indigenous cultures

Human occupation of the American continents took place at a relatively late stage in the evolution of humankind, perhaps as late as
30 thousand years ago. Animal species in African and Eurasian ecosystems, where humans had been evolving for a long time, adapted to
this effective mammal, and in most cases managed to survive. In
America, humans found a different fauna, composed of animals not
adapted to human presence and, frequently, an easy target for the arriving hunters and gatherers. Some of the large mammals (several species
of Glyptodon, Toxodon, Mylodon, and Mastodon) were hunted to
extinction in a few millennia. Therefore, from the beginning, humans
provoked a profound upheaval in American ecosystems.

"Paleo-Indian" groups were soon forced to adapt to the changes
that they themselves had produced. After many generations of migration and technological and social development, the new societies gradually developed sustainable social and environmental models, which, in
general, conserved the main ecosystems without major changes for several millennia. A whole spectrum of cultures evolved in the various
environments of the Americas and, by the time the European conquerors arrived, they were well established throughout the continents.

In the high valleys of the central Andes and Central America,
numerous farming societies were organized into relatively large kingdoms or empires, such as those of the Aztecs in Mexico and the
Tahuantisuyu in Peru. The Mexican states were organized around the
cultivation of corn, chili peppers, and tomatoes, and the raising of
turkeys and dogs. Their capital, at the time of the arrival of the
Spaniards, was the large island-city of Tenochtitlán. The Peruvian
states of western South America based their economy mainly on potato,
corn, and quinoa farming and raising llamas; their capital was the large
Andean city of Cuzco.

In the northern Andes, the high valleys were occupied by agricultural societies (the Chibchas) who had also developed impressive skills

The ruins of Tiwanaco, one of the largest pre-Inca urban centres (in present-day Bolivia), are a reminder of the sophisticated urban societies that prospered in South America before the arrival of the Spanish.

in metallurgy. Chibcha groups were organized into small states ruled by a chieftain.

In the Yucatán and Guatemala, relatively prosperous farming towns have been established by the Mayas, who were in the process of economic and political decline when the Europeans arrived. Several larger towns were abandoned and apparently some of their inhabitants settled in the mountains not far from present-day Guatemala City.

The Caribbean islands had been occupied by many farming and fishing communities — originally the Arawaks, who had been displaced by the Caribs on some islands. Arawaks and Caribs were also present throughout the forests of South America.

The huge South American forests were the territory of the Tupi–Guarani cultures, who gradually became well adapted to these rich, but difficult, ecosystems. The Tupi–Guaranis extended from the Amazon to the Río de la Plata and from the Andes foothills to the Atlantic Ocean. Their subsistence was based on itinerant farming of corn and cassava and various extractive activities, such as hunting, fishing, and the gathering of plants and small animals.

The grasslands of South America were inhabited by nonfarming groups of hunter–gatherer–fishers who lived by hunting the *venado* (a small South American deer), ostriches, and armadillos. These societies were organized politically in small groups and confederations. Similar groups, but larger and better organized politically, existed in the prairies of North America, where they relied on buffalo hunting and other extractive activities.

Finally, the cooler regions at the extremes of the continents were inhabited by various groups of hunters and fishers, such as the Tehuelches, the Onas, and the Fueguinos in Patagonia and Tierra del Fuego at the southern tip of South America, and the Inuit, Dene, and Algonquins in the northern regions of North America.

In general, indigenous societies were adapted to the specific conditions in local ecosystems; the ones that did not adapt, disappeared. In the rain-forest ecosystems, complex land-use systems developed. They included small plots for slash-and-burn farming, specific areas reserved for medicinal plants or animals, and zones for social activities and various religious or "magic" rites. On the whole, this system constituted a sustainable approach to forest management.

In the grasslands, hunting practices included taboos and respect for "totems," ensuring that indiscriminate killing could not endanger the survival of the resource species. Both in southern and in northern grasslands, hunting groups followed the herds, which were extensive. There are many historical references to the huge numbers of buffalo roaming the North American central plains. Similar references exist on the abundance of *venado* in the Uruguayan grasslands; according to the Portuguese explorer, de Souza, in 1532 they "covered the land to the horizon." Their numbers were more or less stable.

Farming activities in the mountain societies were also carried out in a sustainable manner. The farming systems in the Altiplano were (and still are) complex, including cultivation of several different types of crops at the same time and a rotation system, ensuring maximum production without irreversible losses of fertility or incidence of plagues.

The colonial period

After 1492, when the first Spanish expedition arrived, a dramatic change occurred. Before the end of the 15th century, the first Spanish explorers became conquerors, settling in several islands of the Caribbean — Santo Domingo, Hispaniola, Puerto Rico, etc. — and, shortly after this, the Portuguese founded their first colonies in Brazil. In Santo Domingo, the Spaniards treated the indigenous population as slaves, raped native women, and did not hesitate to kill whole communities when they offered resistance. After 50 years of Spanish occupation, only a few hundred indigenous people had survived these genocidal practices and the deadly European diseases. Finally, widespread suicide among the survivors resulted in the early disappearance of these ethnic groups. Similar developments occurred in the other Caribbean islands controlled by the Spaniards. In Brazil, the behaviour of the Portuguese was not much different. Thousands of indigenous people were put to work as slaves, and expeditions set out from the settled areas on the coast into the interior to obtain more labourers.

In the 16th century, the main purpose of the Europeans was to obtain precious metals and gemstones, such as gold, silver, and emeralds. The Spaniards invested much effort in exploiting existing mines and opening new ones. They developed silver and gold mines in Potosí, in upper Peru (present-day Bolivia), Taxco, Mexico, and many other areas. The financial gains from these mining activities funded a massive colonization effort.

Spaniards and Portuguese settlers reproduced the European feudal system in America. The settlers were awarded *encomiendas*, the equivalent of European fiefdoms. The production systems introduced by the Europeans were extractive and damaging. Widespread mineral exploitation and indiscriminate deforestation, overcultivation, and overgrazing without concern for sustainability were the rule. The impact was severe in many areas, and some ecosystems were destroyed beyond repair. Because of the limited number of settlers, however, a major portion of the natural environment remained relatively untouched.

In Andean farming areas, the landowners controlled large numbers of indigenous peasants who continued farming, more or less as before, except for having to work for long periods, sometimes many years, in the mines. In the grasslands, the land was awarded to settlers to raise cattle, which were introduced in southern South America in the 16th century. Cattle replaced the *venado* and other herbivorous prairie animals, some of which became more and more scarce and, in a few cases, came close to extinction.

Exploitation of natural resources after independence

At the beginning of the 19th century, most Spanish colonies declared independence, taking advantage of Spain's preoccupation with Napoleon's invasion of the Iberian peninsula. About 20 new countries were formed in Hispanic America. A few years later, in 1822, the Portuguese colonies in Brazil also became an independent monarchy. Cuba and Puerto Rico remained under colonial rule until the end of the 19th century.

However, the old feudal-style colonial exploitation persisted in the recently formed countries. The new criollo elites were often the largest landowners, and the old social structure remained intact. Large farms and ranches were the successors of the old *encomiendas* and continued producing in much the same way as the old Spanish and Portuguese plantations had.

During the 19th century, countries of Latin America and the Caribbean turned to the processing of various raw materials and food products for export, mainly to Europe and, especially during the last decades of the century, the United States. Exploitation of natural resources was ruthless, with little concern for environmental effects. In areas of high population density, such as mountain valleys or coastal zones, deforestation was intense, mining and quarrying proceeded at an ever faster pace, hunting drove many wild animals to the brink of extinction, and soil erosion was common in farming areas.

In the 20th century, these trends increased. Lands belonging to indigenous peoples were occupied with little recognition of their rights, and environmental damage continued. The economies of Latin American and Caribbean countries, which were export-oriented from colonial times, became even more so because of the establishment of railroads and the growth of major ports.

In Argentina and Uruguay, economic growth was based on beef, leather, wool, and wheat. The railway system of Argentina converged on the main export port, Buenos Aires. This city had grown very quickly in both population and commercial activity. In 1870, it had a population of more than 100 thousand; in the 1950s, it had grown to 8 million people. In Uruguay, the railroad system radiated from Montevideo, the only exporting centre, which also grew rapidly from 50 thousand inhabitants in 1860, to 300 thousand in 1900, to 1 million by 1960. This demographic growth was the result of a continuing influx of immigrants, mainly from Europe, which in large measure determined the ethnic makeup of these cities.

In Brazil, the export market was based in São Paulo and its port, Santos, and in Rio de Janeiro, which was the capital until the 1960s. The main exports from the São Paulo area were coffee, sugarcane, and timber (Brazil pine). From Bahia and the northeast, cocoa, copra,

Brazilian forests — such as Mata Atlantica in Rio Grande do Sul — are being removed at an alarming rate. Today, only a few remnants of this once-great coastal forest remain untouched.

sugarcane, and bananas were exported from the main ports: Salvador and Recife. The Amazon region specialized in the production of rubber, particularly near the port city of Manaus. This product was an important source of revenue for several decades, until the rubber tree was introduced in Malaysia and Brazilian production declined.

Recently, the Amazon has witnessed a widespread gold rush. The *garimpeiros* (small gold miners) have moved into many potentially gold-rich areas, seriously affecting formerly pristine environments. River sediments are dredged and treated with quicksilver (mercury) to separate the gold. Mercury is carried by the rivers and eventually concentrates in plant and animal tissues. In several Amazon rivers, fish systematically show high mercury levels; their human consumers with similar symptoms. In the fishing community of Rainha, on the Tapajoz, hair samples from local villagers have shown mercury levels much higher than the WHO standard maximum of 6 ppm (Serril 1994). Similar conditions are routinely found in the Madeira, Xingu, and Negro subbasins. Amazonian indigenous groups, which largely depend on fish for their survival, are often the first victims of this process of contamination and poisoning.

The Pacific coast countries and Bolivia, which were exporters of precious metals (mainly silver) in colonial times, continued to produce minerals, such as copper and nitrates in Chile and tin in Bolivia. In this region, centralization was less marked. This was primarily because of the region's geography — a long mountain range or ranges bordering narrow coastal plains and valleys. The main export outlets were the two oldest colonial ports: Valparaiso in Chile and Lima, Peru.

In Central America, the Caribbean, and the northern coast of Colombia, the main products were bananas, coffee, and copra. Often, export activities were carried out by American-owned companies that controlled production and access to foreign markets. The United Fruit Company, which was extremely powerful in Cuba, Guatemala, Nicaragua, El Salvador, and Costa Rica, used its influence to change governments or induce American military interventions. The Central American republics at that time were, ironically, called "Banana Republics."

In Mexico, the drive to export was somewhat slowed during the revolution of the 1910s, when dictator Porfirio Díaz was overthrown by a peasant revolution headed by Emiliano Zapata in the south and Pancho Villa in the north. This revolution radically changed the structure of land ownership in the country. By the end of the 1930s, with the nationalization of the petroleum industry by Lazaro Cardenas, Mexico's main export product became nationally owned.

At the same time, the main cities of the continent began developing an important industrial base. In Argentina, Uruguay, and southern Brazil, exporting enterprises, such as textile plants, slaughterhouses, and tanneries developed. In other cases, industries were geared to national markets, and were usually sheltered from foreign competition by protectionist policies. The main industrial cities were Buenos Aires, São Paulo, and Mexico City, but industrial areas also became established in Havana, Santiago, Montevideo, Bogotá, and Lima.

This widespread economic trend toward exports and increasing industrial activities had a very strong effect on the already-damaged Latin American and Caribbean environment. Elimination of the forests and the spread of monospecific plantations increased the vulnerability of soils to water and wind erosion, and hydrological regimes changed everywhere, increasing the frequency of floods and droughts. The increase in urban and industrial activities produced a cumulative deterioration of natural water systems. Small rivers near the cities became open sewers, larger rivers and lakes received considerable volumes of contaminants, and aquifers became saline or polluted.

Effects of globalization on the environment

Recent globalization processes have intensified the widespread degradation. The largest cities hold 10 to 20 million people; industrial activities, previously confined to the agro-exporting sector, have already expanded or are now expanding to other sectors, such as automobile and chemical production. A large-scale invasion of *maquiladora*-type industries is taking place in Mexico, Costa Rica, Guatemala, and the Dominican Republic, with deleterious effects on the environment because of the lack of standards in these countries or their inadequate enforcement.

Macroeconomic trends are promoting deforestation in Mato Grosso, Santa Cruz (Bolivia), and Paraguay to make way for soybean plantations. Chilean native forests are being eliminated to plant exotic trees for production of timber or paper pulp. These new monospecific plantations are responsible for a large number of side effects on native ecosystems and hydrological regimes, resulting in loss of diversity and significant social upheaval.

Grassland ecosystems and associated farmlands are being taken over by huge forestry investments in exotic tree species, which are promoting the spread of new plagues, reducing agricultural competitiveness, and damaging the future potential of prairie soils. Rivers are becoming loaded with sediments as a result of the destruction of ecosystems in their headwaters.

These environmental problems are taking their toll on the quality of life of the populations. Old waterborne diseases, such as cholera, that had disappeared or were largely unknown, have made a startling comeback almost everywhere. The poor air quality in the main metropolitan areas is increasing the incidence of respiratory diseases. Geological hazards, such as landslides and floods, are becoming more frequent because of the encroachment of settlements in hazardous areas.

Models of development in Latin America and the Caribbean have proved to be unsustainable. Alternatives must ensure that economic activities and populations are decentralized, that only sustainable production systems are adopted, and that these systems are based, as much as possible, on indigenous plants and animals.

The exploitation of natural resources should not continue indiscriminately; the biological diversity of native ecosystems must be protected. Adequate policies defining strict environmental standards for the disposal of solid wastes and effluent and gaseous emissions must be formulated and enforced. Overall, everyone must be made aware that other development alternatives, more sustainable, more diverse, and more indigenous, can be successfully defined and implemented.

The *maquiladora* phenomenon

Maquiladoras are offshore plants that carry out part or all of the phases of an industrial process for the parent company. Customs duties charged by the country of origin of the industry are usually calculated only on the value added outside its borders. The host country (where the *maquiladoras* are located) extends free-port status to industries willing to invest. In most cases, this means that the host country does not charge duties (or charges only nominal amounts) on the raw materials, partly completed products, or merchandise related to the specific industrial process when they cross the border in either direction.

Carrying out industrial operations offshore under this system reduces costs of production for the entrepreneur. In appropriate situations, costs of labour, energy, water, raw materials, environmental expenditures, and taxes can be reduced by establishing *maquiladora* factories. This system is being used in various forms in several countries throughout the world, but the major growing *maquiladora* region is probably the United States – Mexico border area.

Development in the border region

The border between Mexico and the United States (Figure 4) extends for more than 1 500 kilometres through a territory of steppes and deserts where, traditionally, the population density was low. Historically, only limited settlement occurred in this zone because its climate is unsuitable for rainfed agriculture and surface water resources are too meagre for use in irrigated farming. Before 1900, except for Ciudad Juárez and Monterrey, there were only a few small towns scattered near the border area; their economic activity was restricted to low-productivity agriculture, marginal animal production, and cross-border trade (both legal and illegal).

During the 20th century, economic and demographic growth in the border area was mainly related to increased traffic and commerce between the two countries, and to the development of irrigated farming projects on both sides of the border. On the Mexican side, the federal government supported drilling and groundwater pumping; on the US side, new water sources were developed by constructing an aqueduct

Figure 4. Maquiladora *country: the border region between Mexico and the United States.*

system from neighbouring rivers. Coupled with the availability of inexpensive migrant labour and cheap land, these improvements allowed the development of a powerful farming industry.

Industrial development began in the 1950s in Monterrey and, in the 1970s and 1980s, in the remaining border areas as a consequence of the *maquiladora* phenomenon. From the outset, these factories had profound effects on the economy and demography of the border region. The populations of existing cities increased rapidly. "Sleepy towns" became large cities in a matter of a few years. The social and environmental impact of this growth continue today.

The metropolitan area of Tijuana, which had a population of 461 thousand in 1980, grew to 748 thousand by 1990 (Secretaría de Desarrollo Social 1993, p. 301). Nearby, Mexicali's population increased from 511 to 602 thousand in the same period; Reynosa's from 295 to 377 thousand; Matamoros' from 239 to 303 thousand; and

Ciudad Juárez's from 567 to 798 thousand. During the 1980s, the number of people in the whole urban border area increased from 2.8 to 3.8 million (Secretaría de Desarrollo Social 1993, pp. 197–198).

The evolution of the *maquiladora* phenomenon is illustrated in Table 7. In 1994, there were more than 2 500 factories providing jobs for 1 million people or about 15% of all those employed in industry in the country. In 1975, the total annual value added by the *maquiladora* industries was $332.4 million; this increased to more than $2.5 billion by early 1989 and, in 1994, it was expected to exceed $5 billion.

Tijuana contains the largest number of *maquiladora* plants; by 1992, 530 industries of this type were located there. Other cities near the Californian border also host a large number of factories: Mexicali, 154; Tecate, 86; Ensenada, 33; and San Luis Colorado, 12. Along the Arizona–Sonora boundary, the main centre is Nogales, with 73 plants. On the Texas border, the main concentrations are in Matamoros, 94; Nuevo Laredo, 83; Reynosa, 71; and Monterrey, 70.

Table 7. *Growth in* maquiladora's *near the US – Mexico border.*

Year	No. factories	No. workers	% of total industrial employment
1975	454	67 214	4.2
1976	448	74 496	4.5
1977	443	78 433	4.8
1978	457	90 704	5.0
1979	540	111 365	5.7
1980	620	119 546	5.4
1981	605	130 923	5.3
1982	585	127 048	5.4
1983	600	150 867	7.6
1984	672	199 864	9.7
1985	760	211 969	—
1986	891	249 833	—
1987	1 125	305 253	—
1988	1 396	369 489	—
1989	1 631	427 244	—

Source: CIDAC (1991, p. 119).

Wages in Mexico are low: in 1992, they averaged $1.22 per hour, compared with $3.67 per hour in South Korea and $4.63 per hour in Taiwan. At the same time, average hourly wages in the United States and Canada exceeded $17 (Bettson 1993). This level of wage differential promotes the "migration" of labour-intensive industries to the inexpensive side of the border.

An additional factor promoting the installation of factories in Mexico is the absence of a powerful trade-union movement there. In effect, the main workers' union, the Confederación de Trabajadores de Mexico, is largely under the control of the governing party (Partido Revolucionario Institucional), making it difficult for industrial workers to organize strikes or press for better working conditions or pay.

In addition, *maquiladoras* tend to hire more women than men. In Mexico, women, who are at a social disadvantage, see the prospect of working in factories as "liberation" from a male-chauvinist society. Entrepreneurs take advantage of this situation. After some time, however, women become tired of the repetitive, nonthinking jobs and long hours. Trade-union movements have begun several times as workers struggle for higher wages, better working conditions, and shorter hours. In response, some companies have simply vacated their premises during a weekend and left the country. This "reduced responsibility" of employers in Mexico is an "advantage" that some industries are using to their benefit.

Environmental problems

According to the environmental report of Secretaría de Desarrollo Social (1993, p. 197), of the 1 929 *maquiladora* plants, only 206 (11%) had treatment systems. In addition, 1 094 plants (57%) emitted pollutants into the atmosphre; 1 254 (65%) of them did not have a system for reducing the contaminant content of their emissions. About 55% of the industrial plants (821) produce hazardous solid wastes. Of the 821 *maquiladoras* operating near the US–Mexico border that generate hazardous wastes, only 71% had reported these wastes by mid-1992.

Maquiladoras are a source of environmental problems for several reasons. First, environmental laws and controls in Mexico are much less

8.
The case of Ciudad Juárez

By late 1992, Ciudad Juárez, in the central border region, contained 330 *maquiladoras*, the second largest concentration in the country (after Tijuana). Because of these industries, the city grew from a medium-sized town of 400 thousand people in the 1970s to twice that number in the early 1990s. Many new suburban neighbourhoods developed, making it difficult for municipal and state authorities to provide essential services. The city is across the Rio Grande from El Paso, Texas, which is also a fast-growing city (with a population of more than 400 thousand).

Before the *maquiladora* revolution, Ciudad Juárez was known for fast divorces and inexpensive dental work. Today, many major US-based, Japanese, and other transnational companies — General Electric, Northern Telecom, Phillips, Toshiba, TDK, Honeywell, and RCA — have factories there.

According to Bettson (1993), the metropolitan area of El Paso is the seventh most polluted metropolitan area in the United States. Atmospheric data show high levels of ozone, sulphur dioxide, carbon monoxide, nitrous oxide, and lead.

The people who are most affected by environmental problems in the Juárez – El Paso region are those living in the new suburbs near the factories. Tuberculosis, hepatitis, skin diseases, gastrointestinal problems, miscarriages, and cancer are all unusually high in these areas compared with the rest of Mexico. Cases of anencephaly (babies born without a brain), normally a rare condition, have become frequent (163 cases in 4 years) and are attributed to exposure to toxic substances used in the *maquiladoras* (Bettson 1993).

strict than in the rest of North America, promoting the relocation of many industries that are looking to reduce costs (not only labour, but also environmental costs). Second, industries experiencing problems with occupational health and safety can expect related costs to decrease when then move south of the border. Finally, the excessive concentration and fast growth of the *maquiladora* cities make it difficult for the Mexican authorities to build or provide the required infrastructure and services (see box 8).

The redistribution of economic roles

The *maquiladora* phenomenon is only one aspect of the effect on Mexico of the world redistribution of economic roles. Some Mexican industrial exports to the United States increased significantly between 1986 and 1989 (Table 8).

Most (over 60%) of the investment behind this industrial expansion, which to a large degree complemented the *maquiladora* phenomenon, originated in the United States. Other countries with interests in Mexico include the United Kingdom (contributing 6.7% of foreign investment in 1989), Germany (6.3%), Japan (5.3%), and Switzerland (4.4%) (CIDAC 1991, p. 165).

According to *El Universal* in Mexico City (Cortés 1993, p. 3), by mid-1993, the *maquiladora* sector had overtaken the petroleum sector as the main generator of foreign currency. The rate of increase in added value as a result of the *maquiladoras* had been 13% for the last 5 months (April to August 1993). During the same period, employment in the factories increased by 9%. By May 1993, the sector provided employment to almost 546 thousand workers. In Baja California alone, where there were 809 plants, inputs to the *maquiladoras* and exporting industries reached $2.7 billion in 1992. For the whole country, the value of inputs was $14 billion, representing a significant contribution to the Mexican economy.

Table 8. Rate of increase (%) in Mexico's exports, 1986 to 1989.

Industry	1986	1987	1988	1989
Automobiles	343	151	7.4	16.1[a]
Machinery	52	40.7	14.8	—
Steel	85.3	42.1	20.5	—
Textiles	71	70.1	10.6	—

Source: CIDAC (1991, p. 146).
[a] To October.

Farming on both sides of the border

These economic trends had an important impact on farming in northern Mexico. California has traditionally been an important farming state. Recently, however, as a result of decreased availability and increased cost of water and labour and environmental restrictions, the state is importing more farm products from Mexico and other Latin American countries, such as Chile. Mexico's exports of fruit to the United States increased by 20.1% in 1986, 30.5% in 1987, and 0.2% in 1988; vegetable exports grew by 22.4% in 1986, 20.2% in 1987, and 12.5% in 1988 (CIDAC 1991).

California has always been a fruit producing and exporting state. The fact that it is now importing some produce from Mexico is striking. The main reason for this trend is the lower cost of labour in Mexico, despite the much higher agricultural yields in the United States. From 1986 to 1988, comparative yields (tonnes per hectare) in the United States and Mexico, respectively, were as follows: potatoes, 33 613 and 13 000; tomatoes (industrial), 56 234 and 25 182; lettuce, 33 396 and 30 360 (Gómez Cruz et al. 1992, p. 52).

Productivity is also generally much lower in Mexico. The difference is particularly evident in the case of some basic grains. To produce 1 tonne of corn, Mexican farmers work 17.84 days, whereas US farmers require only 0.14 days (slightly more than 1 hour of work). Therefore, labour input for corn production is 127 times lower in the United States than in Mexico. Similarly, to produce 1 tonne of beans, it is necessary to work 50.60 days in Mexico, but only 0.60 days in the United States. Rice requires 33.14 days per tonne in Mexico and 0.23 days per tonne in the United States. Wheat production is less demanding in terms of labour: 3.17 days per tonne in Mexico, 0.33 days per tonne in the United States, and only 0.13 days per tonne in Canada (Calva Téllez 1992, p. 27).

Despite the much lower costs for agricultural labour in Mexico, the large differences in productivity are reduced when the actual cost of grain production is calculated; production costs remain substantially higher in Mexico. Producing corn costs $258.62 per tonne in Mexico and only $92.74 per tonne in the United States; for beans, the costs are

$641.17 and $219.53 per tonne respectively. The costs of rice production are not substantially different ($224.20 per tonne in Mexico and
$189.89 per tonne in the United States). Wheat production costs are
much lower in Canada ($93.11 per tonne) than in the United States
($143.71 per tonne) and Mexico ($152.51 per tonne) (Calva Téllez
1992, p. 26).

The cost of producing animal feed is also higher in Mexico. For
example, 1 tonne of sorghum costs $152.79 to produce in Mexico and
$89.25 in the United States; 1 tonne of barley costs $222.09 in Mexico,
$153.50 in the United States, and only $69.95 in Canada; and 1 tonne
of soybeans costs $324.64 in Mexico and $184.26 in the United States
(Calva Téllez 1992, p. 27).

These figures show that, at least for some crops, US farmers are in a
more competitive position than their Mexican counterparts. For many
labour- and water-intensive crops, however, depending on rainfall and
demand, Mexican produce can be marketed at a lower cost than US
products. This is the case for some irrigated crops, such as broccoli and
asparagus, that are normally produced south of the border and sold in
the United States. California's growing scarcity of water is favouring
Mexican encroachment into the US market.

In Mexico, pumping of deep groundwater for irrigation is promoted
by farmers being charged for power at rates far below actual costs. These
rates were introduced by the former president of Mexico, Lazaro
Cardenas, in 1936. They were eliminated in 1992 by C. Salinas, but
reintroduced later as a result of the serious financial problems that its
removal produced among northern farmers.

Pumping costs increase as the level of the water table drops; therefore, the deeper the water level, the greater the subsidy to farmers. This
policy contributes to overuse of aquifers beyond their capacities. In
northern Mexico, there is a risk that some aquifers will be depleted and
some others may deteriorate as saline or other low-quality water enters
them. Inexpensive electricity and federal support for hydroelectric
works are the framework on which agricultural expansion in northern
Mexico is based.

In brief, farming is heavily subsidized by the federal governments on both sides of the border. In the United States, the price of water does not include the cost of the water systems that were built to reach otherwise dry, semi-desert regions. In Mexico, not only are the infrastructures financed by the government, but there is also an additional subsidy extended through artificially low rates for the electricity used for pumping water.

Again, as in other areas of the world, the border region between the United States and Mexico is developing rapidly, but based on very fragile environmental and social models. New and imaginative solutions must be found if this and similar areas are to enjoy a stable and prosperous future.

12

The Urban Environmental Challenge

The development of modern cities

Modern cities are a result of the industrial age. In the 14th and 15th centuries, before the industrial revolution, Venice and Paris were the only European cities whose populations had reached 100 thousand; London, at that time, had a mere 50 thousand inhabitants. Shanghai, the largest city in China, had about 100 thousand people and, Fez, the capital of the Moorish empire, was smaller. Timbuktu in the Sahel contained fewer than 80 thousand people and the populations of the largest American cities, Tenochtitlán and Cuzco, probably did not exceed 100 thousand.

To a large extent, the 16th century Renaissance was the result of the incorporation of large nonecumenical areas of the world into the European "civilized fold" as a result of discovery and the political and military imperialism of the European powers. This trend toward globalization of trade and political might allowed the consolidation of the main European states, as well as the accumulation of enormous financial resources. These, in turn, provided the investments required to begin the industrial revolution.

European cities, which had originally developed as commercial centres, became the sites of the first industrial experiments. Industrial processes required many workers to manipulate the new machines, and gradually thousands of labourers from the impoverished European countryside began moving to the urban areas. By the end of the 18th century, cities had grown considerably: Hamburg grew from 70 thousand in 1700 to about 130 thousand in 1800 and New York from 33 thousand in 1790 to 60 thousand in 1800. The rapid growth did not allow time for urban planning. These cities did not have adequate services, and the quality of life of the working class was poor and unhealthy.

The large industrial megalopolises developed in the 19th century. London was one of the first cities to surpass 1 million people; at the beginning of the 19th century, it had a population of 1.12 million, increasing to 6.59 million by 1901. Paris expanded from 550 thousand people in 1801 to 2.5 million in 1891, and the largest industrial city in North America, New York, which had reached 1 million people by 1870, had a population of 5.6 million in the 1920s. Berlin grew from 830 thousand people in 1871 to 2 million in 1912; Hamburg from 130 thousand in the early 1800s to 700 thousand by 1900; and Cologne from 42 thousand in 1801 to 370 thousand in 1900. In Japan, Tokyo (then Edo) had reached 1.2 million people in the 1850s. By the early 20th century, at least 10 cities in the world contained 1 million inhabitants or more.

During the last decades of the 19th century, some of the most pressing urban environmental problems (water supply and sanitation) were addressed, but many new problems (contamination of rivers and air pollution) continued to develop. This was a time when smog threatened the health of urban dwellers in the industrial world and the stench of the filthy water of the Thames and Hudson rivers pervaded their adjacent cities.

This unprecedented urban growth was related to the competitive edge imparted by industrial production systems. These systems were based on the use of engines of various types running on fossil fuels, and later hydroelectricity, and on complex production methods in which each worker specialized in a specific task while a centralized

Even beautiful Venice is sinking in its own ugly waters.

management oversaw all the steps of the process and ensured their coordination. The new sources of energy and the effectiveness of its use permitted mass production, which, in turn, attracted increasing numbers of rural dwellers to work in city factories or the myriad service activities that were developing as a result of the economic growth.

The bigger-is-better model was applied to all aspects of life: large cities, tall buildings, giant engineering works, huge hospitals, wide highways, large schools, and universities were the rule. The development of a city was measured by the height of its skyscrapers, the length and width of its highways, the size of its factories, and the number of its inhabitants. Quality of life was secondary.

The environmental problems of London and New York at the end of the 19th century had been more or less solved, but new ones kept appearing. Supplying water to so many people became a difficult enterprise. In New York, the aquifers of Long Island were depleted and saltwater intrusion ensued. In London, the Thames became an open sewer. Similar situations could be found in Frankfurt on the polluted Mainz River, Cologne on the Rhine, and Moscow on the Moscova.

Suddenly, solutions had to be found. Urban planners became important people, large investments were made, a drive to decentralize developed (partly as a result of planning, partly spontaneously), and the growth of the industrial urban areas slowed. Today, the populations of the largest European cities are largely stable. In the 1990s, London's population is smaller than it was in the 1950s. The population of Paris peaked at 10 million in the early 1970s and has not increased much in the last two decades. Hamburg's population decreased from 1.85 million in 1965 to 1.7 million by the end of the 1980s. The cores of the largest northeastern American cities (New York, Pittsburgh, Philadelphia, Chicago, etc.) have stopped growing and a new, less-concentrated urban model, more focused on urban development, is taking form.

Large cities in the Third World

Developing countries are experiencing a replay of the industrial experience. The largest Third World cities have welcomed many of the polluting industries that were moving out of developed countries. The large metallurgy factories, automobile-making complexes, chemical industries of various kinds, large tanneries, and many other pillars of the industrial age have begun to sprout up all over the world: in São Paulo, Seoul, Mexico City, Cairo, Bombay, Manila, Djakarta, and many other metropolises.[13]

Whereas the populations of London and New York, the largest megacities of the past, have stabilized, Third World cities are still growing: Mexico City has 20 million people; São Paulo, 18 million; Shanghai, Cairo, Bombay, and Calcutta, 15 million each; Seoul and Buenos Aires, 12 million; Manila, Bangkok, Djakarta, and Rio de Janeiro, 10 million. The list is not complete. According to the old industrial standard, London, Paris, and Frankfurt have fallen behind — but have they? Perhaps, the population of cities only measures their degree of unsustainability. Perhaps, the higher ranking cities are the ones with less time to change direction.

---

[13] Anton (1993) presents an in-depth study of environmental problems in the megacities of Latin America.

*Garbage recycling is a vital activity for the largest cities of India,
such as Bombay (shown here).*

The megacities of today

Many cities of 10 or more million people concentrated in a relatively small area are trying to survive. Some, such as Tokyo and Los Angeles, are in the "old" industrial countries. However, the majority are found in the Third World. Some of the problems they are experiencing are representative of the challenges affecting all urban areas today.

Mexico: a thirsty city[14]

There are few cases in the world in which the physical environment has been so completely transfigured by urban development as it was in Mexico City. The valley of Mexico is a 9 600 square kilometre closed basin that is more than 2 200 metres above sea level, in the heart of the Mexican neovolcanic belt. Before the arrival of Europeans in 1521, the

---

[14] Material in this section is based on Herrera et al. (1982), Castillo Berthier (1983), Granados Velazco (1988), Ortega (1988), Cortés et al. (1989), Gonzalez Moran and Rodriguez Castillo (1989), Herrera (1989), and Ryan (1989).

valley was a depression in whose bottom several large lakes had developed because of volcanic obstruction of their outlets about 700 thousand years ago. The lakes covered a total area of about 2 thousand square kilometres and were partly connected, especially during periods of high water. Three of the lakes contained fresh water — Chalco, Mexico, and Xochimilco — and the other three, brackish water — Ecatepec, Texcoco, the largest at 800 square kilometres, and Zumpango.

The area was, and to a certain extent still is, subhumid. Rainfall was probably slightly more than the current amount, which ranges from 600 millimetres per year at the bottom of the valley to 1 200 millimetres per year in the nearby mountains. The average temperature was relatively cool for the subtropic latitude at which the city is located, ranging from 8° to 15°C depending on the altitude. Soils were deep, highly fertile, and easy to work.

The land was completely covered by thick forests, particularly on the slopes of the mountains and highland areas. The plains in the valley, which were originally also covered by forests, were soon allocated for agriculture, and parts of the forest were cleared to make way for farms. In addition to the freshwater lakes, a large number of springs around the lakes and in the foothills of the nearby mountains provided considerable volumes of good-quality water.

Because of its abundant resources, the valley was occupied early by a number of indigenous peoples, who based their economy on locally domesticated crops and farm animals: corn, tomatoes, chili peppers, cacao, turkeys, dogs, honey bees, and fish. Because these people did not have draft animals or use the wheel, most trade was carried out by boat (or walking).

Several peoples successively inhabited and established political control over the lacustrine area during the few centuries before the arrival of the Europeans. The last group was the Aztecs, who arrived from the legendary land of Aztlán (probably in the northern arid territories) during the 14th century.

The Aztecs probably maintained a livelihood by fishing and trading with neighbouring groups. Gradually, they managed to build an island in the centre of the Lake of Mexico on which a town developed: Tenochtitlán. Through alliances and wars, the Aztecs built an empire, and Tenochtitlán became a thriving city of several hundred thousand people. A bridge was built to connect the island with the mainland, and large boats transported people and merchandise. The Aztecs also built earth dikes to control flooding and to separate the brackish lakes from the fresh water. Aqueducts carried fresh water from springs to the city through the lake and along the dikes.

It is difficult to comprehend the extent of the changes that took place in the few centuries after the Spanish conquest. Today, the proud Tenochtitlán has disappeared, and only scattered archaeological remnants can be found. In its place stands the highly urbanized downtown area of Mexico City.

The Lake of Mexico is gone. In its place are several hundred square kilometres of urban neighbourhoods built on what used to be the lake bottom. A few canals and small lakes are the only remnants of Chalco and Xochimilco lakes. Like the southern lakes, the three northern lakes were gradually drained (beginning in 1786), and the former Texcoco Lake has become a vast flat plain on which little vegetation grows because of the highly alkaline soil (pH is over 10). An intricate maze of wells and pipes pump brine from the lacustrine sediments for sodium carbonate and sodium chloride extraction.

The old springs that provided water to the riverine populations are also gone. Now over 5 thousand wells draw more than 50 cubic metres of water per second from an average depth of 100 metres, causing the level of water in the aquifers to subside by as much as 1 metre per year. As a result of this overpumping and the compaction of the upper layers of sediments, widespread subsidence is occurring. The surface has dropped 6 metres in several places and, because of differential rates of subsidence, many structures have been weakened. This phenomenon has been exacerbated by frequent seismic activity, of which the most recent destructive example was the earthquake of September 1985.

The forests that used to cover the adjacent hills have practically disappeared, and widespread soil erosion occurs. Most former agricultural land has been covered by pavement, houses, and other urban constructions. Quarries, which supplied construction materials, can be found throughout the region. Some have become garbage dumps, into which some of the annual 10 million tonnes of garbage is thrown. A significant portion of the garbage is dumped on the "shores" of the former Texcoco Lake, particularly in the south. Ciudad Netzahuatcoyotl, in that area, is a neighbourhood of 3 million people. Although recently established, this urban area is extremely degraded; developed areas alternate with garbage dumps and slums.

Water, which used to flow into the lakes, is channeled out of the basin, together with urban wastewater, through a system of canals and tunnels into the Gulf of Mexico hydrographic system. A number of pumping wells used to supply the city are located next to the canal (the Chalco Canal). Risks of contamination are obvious and, in fact, some wells had to be closed because of the presence of nitrates in the water.

The atmosphere of the valley has also changed. Emissions from 4 million vehicles and 25 thousand industrial establishments in a poorly oxygenated environment (because of the altitude) have transformed the air in Mexico City into one of the most unhealthy urban environments for human life, particularly near the downtown core.

Mexico City contains 21 million people, making it the largest urban centre in the world. Every year, its population increases by 750 thousand people, including both births and migration from the rest of the country. By the year 2000, the city will hold 29 million people (surpassing the population of Canada) and, by 2010, 38 million. If corrective measures are not taken, the city's problems will continue to grow, and the ancient paradise may become one of the worst environmental nightmares of the 21st century.

The aquifer underlying the valley of Mexico is one of the key natural elements in Mexico's environment. It provides the bulk of the water that makes the existence of the city possible. Although some water is brought in from the Lerma–Cutzamala basin, the volume is less than one-fifth of total requirements.

Any other option for bringing water from outside the valley is becoming impractical or too expensive. The Lerma–Cutzamala resources are almost exhausted, but using other basins (such as the

Balsas basin or the Amacuzac subbasin) may mean pumping water 1 200 to 1 500 metres upward and constructing long pipelines, storage reservoirs, and other expensive engineering works. Bringing this water into Mexico City will also deprive a number of communities that now depend on it for irrigation and other uses.

Mexico's aquifer is contained in a number of Tertiary and Quaternary units with a thickness ranging from a few hundred metres to nearly 2 thousand metres. These units comprise a wide range of sedimentary materials. Continued volcanic activity produced huge volumes of pyroclastic material, which has been more or less reworked by fluvial action, and intercalated lava flows. During periods of volcanic activity, tuffs, breccias, ashes, and lava formed; at other times, alluvial and lacustrine action was more important. The main water-bearing layers are the Tarango formation and associated alluvia and the Cenozoic sequence of fractured pyroclastic and lava flows. These are covered by younger lacustrine sediments, confining the main aquifer.

The whole sequence can be up to 2 000 metres thick, but the lower 1 500 metres are more consolidated and less porous. The upper few dozen metres of the aquifer are too close to the upper lacustrine clays and continued pumping might produce dewatering and consolidation of these clays, causing subsidence. Therefore, the usable portion of the aquifer is generally between 100 and 500 metres underground.

The aquifer is recharged mainly in the mountain region (Sierra Chichinautzin in the south, Sierra Las Cruces in the west, and Sierra Nevada to the east). The total available recharge volume has been estimated to be 25 to 50% of precipitation: 25% in Sierra Las Cruces, 35% in Sierra Nevada, and 50% in Sierra Chichinautzin. Of these volumes, about half flows toward the valley of Mexico and the rest outward to other basins. An accurate figure for inflow to the aquifer itself is difficult to estimate (probably 30 to 40 cubic metres per second). However, it is certainly below 50 cubic metres per second — the amount being pumped out — because the water level is sinking.

Additional lowering of water levels will increase inflow from the Sierras because of an increase in gradient. This will not compensate for the deficit, however, particularly if pumping is increased. Precise forecasting of the aquifer's reaction to prolonged extraction requires accurate modeling. Only recently has adequate information on the geometry and hydraulic properties of the reservoir been available. Modeling of the aquifer has been carried out at the Instituto de Geofísica, and it is expected to allow prediction of the actual potential of the groundwater resources of the valley.

It has recently become clear that the groundwater resources of the valley of Mexico are limited and that additional water will have to come from external sources. Such external sources are all found at elevations lower that that of the city. Therefore, tapping this water will not only require enormous energy consumption but will also deprive downstream communities of this vital resource. The bottom line is that the urban model of Mexico City is unsustainable. It has become too large for its territorial base. The city has not only run out of water, but also its air is heavily polluted, the local ecosystems have been destroyed or critically damaged, and the surrounding soils are under severe strain as a result of heavy urbanization. To check this continuous destruction of resources, radical policy shifts are essential. The window of opportunity to save Mexico City is rapidly closing.

Los Angeles: setting priorities

Los Angeles, which was founded by the Spaniards in the 18th century, contained only 1 600 people in 1848. The population was half Spanish and half indigenous peoples and it was twice the size of San Francisco's. In the 1850s, when San Francisco became one of the largest cities of the United States, with more than 50 thousand people and one of the busiest ports in the world, Los Angeles remained a torpid little town. Too far from the gold fields, sitting on an arid plain, and lacking a port and a railroad, it did not possess the conditions for rapid growth.

In the 1860s, Mormons started growing fruits and other vegetables in the area. Later, agriculture was firmly established by Quakers and German farmers. Groundwater was easily accessible and abundant; artesian pressure threw it 2 to 3 metres into the air. In 1867, when a railroad line was established, the city began to grow.

California's Sierra Nevada mountain range blocks moist air coming from the ocean and annual precipitation may vary from 2 400 millimetres on the western slopes to 300 millimetres or less on the east. Rivers flowing west are substantial; those on the east are small, except for the Owens River. The Owens River arises southeast of Yosemite, flows west and south into the Owens Valley, then into highly saline Owens Lake. The region contained a rich ecosystem; shrimp and flies provided food for millions of waterfowl. In the 1860s, the Paiute Indians were practicing irrigation learned from the Spaniards. By the 1870s, settlers had displaced them, taking over the farms and irrigation systems. By the end of the century, 15 to 20 thousand hectares was under cultivation.

When the water supply in Los Angeles became insufficient, one of the first alternative sources to be considered was the Owens River. It was almost 400 kilometres away, but it could provide water for 1 million people — at least that was what the founders of the Los Angeles City Water Company thought at the time. In 1880, however, an expensive engineering project of this type was not possible, and the idea was not acted upon. By 1900, the population had reached 100 thousand, and the artesian pressure of the aquifer supplying their water continued to drop. In 1904, the municipal government took over the city's water company and the LA Department of Water and Power (LADWP) was created. One of its first tasks was to try to secure water rights in the Owens Valley and construct an aqueduct to the city.

City officials also wanted to use excess water from the Owens Valley to irrigate land in the San Fernando Valley. The words of Theodore Roosevelt give us an idea of the ideology of the times: "It is a hundred, or a thousandfold more important to state that this water is more valuable to the people of Los Angeles than to the Owens Valley."

The aqueduct took 6 years to build, up to 6 thousand workers were involved in the enterprise, and it was 360 kilometres long, of which 80 kilometres was in tunnels. More than 190 kilometres of railroad track and 800 kilometres of roads and trails had to be constructed. Up to 380 kilometres of telephone lines and 270 kilometres of power transmission lines were installed. It was a huge undertaking for the time.

During the next 20 years, however, no water from Owens Valley went to Los Angeles. It was all used for irrigation in the San Fernando Valley. From fewer than 1 400 hectares in 1913, the area of irrigated land increased to 35 thousand hectares in 1918. In the 1920s, a drought necessitated the construction of several complementary reservoirs.

In the early 1920s, Los Angeles began to use water from Owens Valley. It was then that the problems began. The city managed to buy most of the remaining water rights, depriving local farmers of the vital resource. At the same time, the drought was becoming serious. In 1923, total rainfall was 250 millimetres; in 1924, 150 millimetres; in 1925, 175 millimetres. In addition, the city's population had grown beyond all expectations over the last decade to 1.2 million. The increased need for water forced Los Angeles authorities to continue buying water rights. The conflict between the city and the farmers became nasty and violent. In 1924, at the height of the drought, the farmers remaining in the Owens Valley flooded their land to stop water from entering the aqueduct. By 1927, terrorist actions had started; large pipes and sections of the aqueduct were dynamited. Roadblocks, car searches, and floodlights transformed the valley into a giant penitentiary.

When the crisis continued, the head of the LADWP, William Mulholland, decided to enlarge an existing dam in the nearby San Francisquito Canyon. In 1928, the storage capacity of the San Francis dam was increased to 4 million cubic metres. The work was no sooner finished than the dam started to leak. Soon after, it collapsed. A wave, 60 to 70 metres high, hit 160 men sleeping downstream in a construction camp and 75 families were killed in San Francisquito Canyon. Where the canyon opens onto the plain, the wave was still 25 metres high and engulfed the village of Castaic Junction. The death toll was about 450.

Finally, a new dam in Long Valley, on the Owens River, was built. By the 1930s, the farming and ranching community of Owens Valley ceased to exist. The last rancher left in the 1950s. Later, several other megaprojects were built, the Colorado was "tamed," and two giant aqueducts were constructed to transfer water from the Colorado Valley to the California valleys and Los Angeles.

In the 1950s and 1960s, large hydroprojects continued to be constructed. The largest one, in the Central Valley, was proposed to supply Los Angeles. However, the real purpose was to increase the value of desert land and the wealth of a few speculators. The Central Valley project is depicted in the film *Chinatown*. As soon as the project was approved, the value of the land increased severalfold. Not a single drop of the water from the Central Valley aqueduct reached Los Angeles. It was used to supply inexpensive irrigation water to farmers. However, despite the dams and aqueducts, overpumping of the valley's aquifers did not stop. Groundwater levels continued to drop and soon new megaprojects were being discussed.

A similar situation had developed on the coastal plains next to the metropolitan area of Los Angeles. In this area, more imaginative approaches were being considered to increase water availability. Instead of investing huge sums of money in distant projects, Los Angeles and Orange counties preferred better management of nearby water resources, especially by increasing recharge into the aquifer by artificial means. Today, in Orange County, groundwater recharge through the bed of the Santa Ana River satisfies 70% of the needs of its 3 million inhabitants. In Los Angeles, a similar solution has been implemented in the Los Angeles River. Neighbouring cities of southern California, such as San Diego, do not have available groundwater and depend almost exclusively on imported water.

Water has been, and still is, a key issue in the urbanization of southern California. However, as difficult as it seems, it is only one aspect of a much larger issue: the development model that has been applied in that region. Water scarcity, poor air quality (see also Chapter 8), soil degradation, and ecosystem destruction have made southern California a veritable urban nightmare. Drastic measures will be needed to begin the healing process. If Los Angeles is to survive, a sustainable and long-term development strategy is needed; and this will require a profound rethinking of southern California's future.

Calcutta: a matter of survival

Calcutta, on one of the branches of the Ganga delta, the Hooghly
River, is strategically located 130 kilometres from the mouth of this
river in the Bay of Bengal in an area of commercial transshipment from
sea to river and land. Although a village named Calcutta existed in the
area in the 16th century, it was not until the end of the 17th century
that the English East India Company established the trading post that
was going to become the current megalopolis. This post was in direct
competition with the upstream river port of Hooghly, controlled by the
Mughals. The site of Calcutta was also selected because it was downstream of the Dutch and French settlements and protected by the
Hooghly River to the west and three brackish lakes on the east.
However, the site was far from ideal from a physical point of view. It is
on a low, hot, humid floodplain no more than 10 metres above sea
level. Calcutta's environment is subtropical, with average temperatures
of about 22°C and rainfall in excess of 1 500 millimetres per year, concentrated in a relatively short period of 4 months (June to September).

The trading post grew relatively quickly, as merchants arrived from
nearby Satgaon and the Mughal emperor decreed freedom of trade in
1717, which encouraged many tradesmen to move to the city. By 1706,
the population was already over 10 thousand; in 1752, it reached
115 thousand; and in 1822, it was 300 thousand, becoming one of the
largest cities in India. By the beginning of the 20th century, the city
contained 1 million people and 10 million in 1975. In 1991, its population was estimated to be 15 million, and it is expected to exceed 20 million before the end of this decade.

The metropolitan area is principally confined to two strips, 5 to
8 kilometres wide, on both sides of the river. The Salt Lake project,
which reclaimed the lowlands on the northeast fringe of the city, was
followed by other local projects allowing lateral expansion of the urban
conglomerate.

Throughout most of its history, the city obtained water from wells
and the Hooghly River, which in 1947 was supplying 75% of the
required water. This stream provided fresh water during the rainy season
and brackish water during the dry period. However, contamination of

the river from urban sources has become so acute that, today, the water is unusable for most purposes. However, many riverine neighbourhoods still use it directly. Since construction of the Farakka barrage in the Ganges, a substantial volume of water is obtained from this surface source. The rest comes from about 200 large wells, some of which were drilled during colonial times.

Although the city needs an estimated 3 million cubic metres of water per day (assuming a low per-capita consumption of 200 litres per day), the actual supply is about half that amount. This deficit has pushed many citizens to drill or excavate their own wells, adding to the strain on groundwater resources.

Unfortunately, no attempts have been made to develop a comprehensive plan to manage the groundwater resources of the city. In fact, even the detailed underground structure of the aquifers is unclear. The major water-bearing horizons are sandy (coarse and medium) with occasional gravel. In the north of the city, these layers are found at a depth of between 46 and 137 metres, dipping toward the south, where they lie between 187 and 274 metres below the surface. In the Calcutta region, these layers are covered by a confining clay layer, which disappears about 50 kilometres north of the city.

The quality of the groundwater is medium to poor. It has a relatively high lime content and total dissolved solids (TDS) values between 500 and 2 000 ppm (hard water). The salinity increases toward the south and east because of the proximity of the Bay of Bengal, and it may become too hard for drinking. In the north and west, the problem is less noticeable. It also has a relatively high iron content, which together with the lime causes corrosion in well tubing and screens and in industrial equipment.

Recharge to the aquifer does not seem to occur under the urban area, fortunately, because of the presence of the impenetrable clay layer. It is believed that it takes place by infiltration in the sandy deposits located near the surface toward the north and west of the city. It is essential to identify and protect these areas to prevent contamination that could irreversibly harm the underground reservoir.

The city contains about 700 kilometres of sewers and about the same length of surface drains. Domestic and human wastes are improperly disposed of in all areas where there are no sewers, contaminating the river. As mentioned, contamination of the groundwater is less likely. However, there are indications that the Farakka barrage is receiving an excessive volume of wastes (urban and agricultural). The Ganga River basin receives practically untreated wastes from a population of 300 million and nearly 1 million square kilometres of active agricultural land. This will affect the quality of the water and increase treatment costs.

For some time, Calcutta has been one of the least healthy cities in the world because of the mismatch between population growth and investment in infrastructure. Calcutta is probably one the first urban nightmares of the Third World, one of the largest cities without the resources it needs to maintain the influx of people. Although degradation of Calcutta's environment has been somewhat slowed recently, the situation remains precarious. Considerable investment and intelligent and imaginative planning will be necessary to transform the city into a liveable place for the majority of its population.

Cairo: the desert megacity

Cairo developed in a fragile environment. With an average annual rainfall of barely 20 millimetres, it depends almost exclusively on water from the Nile River, which crosses the city in an approximate south–north direction. The Nile valley is relatively narrow, seldom more than 20 kilometres wide, and frequently less than 5 kilometres. The valley has developed as the floodplain of the river, and these flatlands have been the site of development of an ancient agricultural civilization that has occupied the region continuously from the time of the Pharaohs (2 to 3 thousand years BC).

The region's economy was (and still is, to a large extent) based on the use of the river waters and sediments for irrigation and fertilization. Since the construction of the Aswan High Dam in 1960, the level of the river has been stable, and flooding no longer occurs. Although the Nile still provides water, the supply of nutrients and sediments has been significantly reduced, and Egyptian farmers are increasingly dependent on (imported) fertilizers.

The Nile widens significantly about 100 kilometres from the Mediterranean Sea. In this area, the riverbed separates into two main canals (the Rosetta and Damietta canals) and many more smaller canals forming a delta-shaped alluvial region. The city of Cairo was established a few kilometres upstream from the widening portion of the valley. This site was repeatedly selected as an urban centre: the Giza pyramids were built (2500–2700 BC) to the west of the river; later, the city of On was founded as a commercial and religious centre for the worship of Ra to the east, where Masr Gadid or New Cairo now stands. Although there were Persian and Roman forts (Babylon) on the site of Old Cairo, the city did not gain importance until the arrival of the Arabs in the 7th century, when the town of Fustat was founded, gradually extending to Askar and Katai. Almost three centuries later, the town of al Qahira was founded in a neighbouring site and, under Saladin, the four locales were united into a larger city.

The city has grown considerably since then. In 1991, there were nearly 14 million people living permanently in the metropolitan area, which extends 80 kilometres, north–south, from al-Matariyah to al-Ma'adi, and more than 15 kilometres on each side of the river, particularly toward the northeast.

Cairo has been built on a plain that lies over alluvial silt–clay deposits about 10 metres thick. Under these deposits is a 60-metre thick, water-bearing sandy formation, which, in turn, covers Mesozoic limestones outcropping toward the south of the urban region.

For centuries, the Nile has been (and continues to be) the main source of water for the people of Egypt and upstream nations. Its waters are abundant and, since construction of the Aswan Dam, shortages do not occur. Wells are used by more distant and isolated communities. Currently, water from the river is treated in three plants, which supply only a portion of the 3 million cubic metres per day needed by the large metropolitan population. More than 3 million people in Cairo have no access to the urban water-supply system, and must buy their water from the carriers (or obtain it directly from the river or shallow wells). The number of households not connected to the system is likely to increase as the population increases. By the end of the century, as many as 5 million people will not be served by the city's water-distribution network.

Before 1980, wastewater and sewage flowed regularly in the low-lying streets of the city. In the early 1980s, the system was gradually reconstructed, but at the end of the decade more than 1 million cubic metres of untreated raw sewage was still entering the river; slightly less than half of the total 2 million cubic metres of wastewater per day was treated. The disposal of untreated sewage into natural systems is causing the spread of waterborne diseases, especially diarrhea, and increasing the risk of cholera and typhoid. Filtration plants are inadequate to process the increasingly polluted Nile waters.

The gravity of the issue has pushed national authorities and international agencies into solving some of the most pressing problems. In 1980, an overhaul of the old system was started (Bedding 1989). The sewers were clogged with dust, dirt, and garbage. As much as 43 thousand tonnes of muck, untreated industrial wastes, and other substances and residues were removed from 57 kilometres of sewers over a 6-year period.

A new system is currently under construction, but will not be finished until well into the next decade (perhaps 2005). Digging in Cairo is an archaeological endeavour. No one knows exactly what is buried under the streets and buildings of the city. Old pipes, graves, ancient buildings, buried tunnels, and walls require careful excavation, which has to be carried out laterally at a depth of more than 25 metres below ground level. This work is partly completed, and when the system is finished, 25 cubic metres per second will be moved toward a treatment plant that will be built 15 kilometres from the city. The plan also includes a large 5 metre diameter tunnel to collect the sewage for later treatment, a pumping station, and effluent canals.

Another problem affecting the city is the rise in the water level in its aquifer, which creates problems during all tunneling operations and for some city basements, and is threatening to cause flooding in low-lying areas. Only a small proportion of the water recharging the aquifer is believed to come from surface rainfall. Because groundwater levels are higher than the Nile River, it is not a source for the aquifer. The most likely sources of recharge seem to be the following:

- Leakage from the water-distribution system;
- Leakage from the sewage system;
- Uncontrolled disposal of wastewater; and
- The return flow of irrigation water.

The partial solution to the problem has been to pump water out of the aquifer into the river. In 1979, nearly 300 thousand cubic metres per day was transferred, but that was insufficient at that time. Additional pumping may be necessary to bring groundwater down to manageable levels.

Cairo is drowning in its own population and wastes. The fragile environment, the lack of precipitation, its dependence on a single water source (which is also the disposal site), and the continuing growth of the city will force the investment of large sums of money to keep the situation even partly under control. The only final solution would be to put a halt to Cairo's growing population, something that would require a drastic review of the current Egyptian development model.

São Paulo: giant of the Third World[15]

Despite its relatively small area by Brazilian standards (245 thousand square kilometres), the State of São Paulo, with 33 million inhabitants, contains about 23% of the country's population at a density that is among the highest in Latin America — almost 140 people per square kilometre. The state also produces over 65% of the industrial output of the country and is the largest agricultural producer; its sugarcane, coffee, and citrus fruit plantations are the largest in Brazil and among the largest in the world. Its cattle stock number nearly 12 million, and it is the biggest producer of milk and dairy products.

The population is mainly urban (over 80%); 29 cities have populations exceeding 100 thousand. The largest, the capital of the state, is

---

[15] Material in this section was drawn from Gardner (1977), Hermann (1979), DAEE (1988), and Mariani Neto et al. (1988).

the city of São Paulo, with 17.5 million inhabitants in early 1990. The 37 municipalities forming the greater São Paulo metropolitan area hold 55% of the population of the state and 15% of the total population of Brazil. The São Paulo urban area alone produces more industrial goods than the rest of the country. More jobs, by far, are created in São Paulo than in any other major city in Brazil. It is not surprising, then, that the city's population has increased through constant immigration from other areas of the country. If current trends continue, greater São Paulo will hold 20 to 22 million people by the year 2000 and 25 to 30 million by 2010.

Portuguese settlement in the São Paulo region began in 1532, when Martin Alfonso de Souza founded the city of São Vicente on the Atlantic coast about 400 kilometres south of the bay of Rio de Janeiro. In that part of the country, the coastal area is a narrow plain at the foot of the Serra do Mar escarpment, with little room for agricultural expansion. Therefore, a settlement was needed in the interior, beyond the coastal mountains. The city of São Paulo de Piratininga or São Paulo dos Campos (which was to become simply São Paulo) was founded in 1554 on a hill between the Anhangabau and Tamanduatei rivers, tributaries of the Tietê.

During the 17th and 18th centuries, the growth of São Paulo was linked with its role as a centre for native workers for the sugarcane plantations of the northeast and for mineral exploration in the hinterland. In the 19th century, the city became a centre for coffee production, which would be the main export of the region and the country for many decades. During the 20th century, particularly during the last few decades, the city's industries grew, producing both for national consumption and for export. Some of the most important industrial activities include metallurgy, automobile manufacturing, chemicals, textiles, and food.

The area's climate is humid subtropical; the average annual temperature is 20°C, varying from an average low of 14°C in winter (July) to an average high of 26°C in the summer (January). São Paulo is among the most humid areas of Brazil. Average annual rainfall ranges from

1 500 to 2 000 millimetres, and can reach 3 000 millimetres in some neighbouring hilly areas.

Although the city of São Paulo is in a high rainfall area, the volume of available water is limited because of the proximity of the Serra do Mar divide. All rivers are small, with small catchment basins, and many dams had to be built to store the water required by this megacity. Unfortunately, groundwater resources are not very abundant either. São Paulo is located on the crystalline Brazilian shield with few hydrogeologically productive areas. The main aquifers in the region are in the coarser sandy lenses of the São Paulo formation and the thick mantle of weathered crystalline rocks. The wells in the city are normally screened at a depth of 100 to 200 metres and can deliver 50 to 1 700 litres per minute.

In its early days, the city's water supply was brought from several surface sources and springs by water carts of doubtful sanitary condition (Avelima 1990). In 1877, when the city's population was about 50 thousand, the private Companhia Cantareira de Esgotos was created to manage the water supply and sanitation. Ten years later, as a result of popular dissatisfaction with this company, the government took it over, forming the Repartição de Agua e Esgotos (RAE). In 1897, the water from the Tietê River already showed signs of contamination and, in 1914, a typhoid epidemic broke out in the poor neighbourhoods of the city.

Originally, all of São Paulo's water drained toward the Paraná basin. In 1920, however, a reservoir was built in the upper Pinheiro basin (the Billings reservoir) to take advantage of the elevation of the Serra do Mar to produce hydroelectric power and water was pumped into it from the Pinheiro River. At that time, this river was not contaminated, because the expanding city had not yet reached its banks. Since then, however, it has become an "open sewer," containing highly contaminated urban wastewaters and storm runoff, which are being pumped into the Billings reservoir.

Instead of discontinuing use of the reservoir for the city's water supply, it has been divided in two parts: one that receives water from the Pinheiro and a smaller section from which water is taken to supply the large suburb of San André (with over 1 million inhabitants) and other urban and suburban neighbourhoods. The two sections are separated by a relatively permeable earth dam; however, the "water supply" is kept at a higher level than the contaminated water to restrict flow into it. Unfortunately, the Billings reservoir also probably receives polluted water from urban areas encroaching on its basin. Close monitoring of the situation is necessary to prevent the obvious hazards.

The upper course of the Tietê River, near and downstream from São Paulo, has also become highly contaminated. Its waters are used to irrigate vegetable farms, which supply São Paulo, then continue downstream through the "Paulista" hinterland, where they supply several communities of the interior. Several attempts to improve this situation have failed, and to correct it now would require a huge capital investment that is not readily available.

In 1973, water management in the area was consolidated under a new body, the Companhia de Saneamento Básico do Estado de São Paulo (SABESP). SABESP has made improvements from an organizational point of view. However, the growth of the metropolitan area has been faster than the expansion of water and sanitation services and, as a result, such services in many urban and suburban areas are inadequate. In a number of communities and in many industrial plants, groundwater is used; as many as 30% of the homes in greater São Paulo obtain their water from wells.

The main water supply for the city and neighbouring municipalities is delivered from a complex network of reservoirs in many small tributaries in the upper basin of the Tietê River, including the Billings reservoir in the upper Pinheiro basin. A complex system of pipes, tunnels, and storage tanks has been constructed to bring water into São Paulo. In 1990, total water consumption in the greater São Paulo area was 50 to 55 cubic metres per second. By the year 2000, it is expected to reach 65 to 70 cubic metres per second; by 2010, 80 to 85 cubic metres per second — exceeding the ultimate capacity of the city's systems.

These estimates are for water obtained from surface sources and do not include private wells. Some groundwater is obtained for municipal use from aquifers contained in the São Paulo formation and in the weathered mantle of a crystalline complex. By far, the main users of groundwater (slightly more than one-third) are industries, which consume 20 to 25 cubic metres per second.

São Paulo will face a difficult future unless plans are made to manage its water resources more carefully. Although its environment was suitable to satisfy the needs of a small or medium-sized city, it is inadequate to provide water to a megalopolis of nearly 20 million people.

13

Diversity and Human Survival

....

In earlier chapters, we examined the widespread processes of environmental degradation that are taking place throughout the world and tried to understand their causes, past and present, as well as the effects that new trends will have on the environment in the years to come. The effects of human action have been profound and cumulative. Earth's atmosphere is being modified, introducing uncertainties about potential consequences, which could be life threatening. Water is being contaminated on every continent, in coastal areas, and even in the open ocean. Simultaneously, the principal fish species are being exploited far beyond replacement levels, introducing profound disturbances in the main aquatic ecosystems. Elimination of vegetation is promoting widespread erosion, changes in hydrological regimes, and, frequently, floods and droughts in areas in which they were previously unknown. "Scars" that are often irreversible are being produced by mining operations, as well as by quarrying for building construction or engineering works such as highways or dams.

The combined effects of these processes are affecting many species of plants and animals, which are finding it increasingly difficult to survive in a changing environment to which they have not had time to adapt. As a result of human activity, the equilibrium of ecosystems is

being altered and widespread modifications of their species composi-
tions and interspecific relations are taking place. A main consequence
of the deterioration of the physical and biological support of ecosystems
is the general loss of biodiversity — both number of species and
varieties.

Along with this biological impoverishment, social and economic
standardization are rapidly reducing the richness of the world's hundreds
of cultures and resulting in the loss of a huge volume of knowledge
about nature that has been accumulated over many generations.
Macroeconomic trends are forcing local communities into high-produc-
tivity, monospecific agriculture or raising animals for commercial purposes, replacing the enormous range of traditional crop and animal
varieties by a few that meet the conditions for short-term competitiveness imposed by globalized international markets.

In much the same way in which species and varieties are becoming
extinct, languages, beliefs, traditions, empirical knowledge, and whole
environmental-management systems are being wiped from the face of
the Earth by a shortsighted, mainstream culture that does not offer
appropriate substitutes for the sustainable long-term strategies that are
often part of the older and more experienced cultures.

The human and biological diversity that is under attack represents
the bulk of the planet's natural and human resource base; reducing
diversity will result in a gradual loss of options for the future, not only
for the current generations, but also for the many to come.

Documenting diversity

In most cases, it is difficult to acquire precise knowledge about species
diversity. Although it is possible to survey plants or animals living in
restricted areas — a few square metres, for example — it is impossible to
survey all plants and animals in larger ecosystems or to decipher the
complex web of their interrelations. Usually, only the main (larger,
more frequent) species and a few varieties are catalogued.

Entomologists believe that there are several million insect species,
perhaps as many as 500 thousand species of Choleoptera. The number
of varieties of these species can run to a hundred million or more.

High-diversity ecosystems, such as the rain forests and coral reefs, are poorly understood. There are often more than 100 species of trees in 1 hectare of Amazon or New Guinea rain forest and perhaps as many as 200 species of molluscs in 1 square kilometre of Australia's Great Barrier Reef. The task of the taxonomist is a slow and difficult one, and it will take centuries before a significant portion of the Earth's biota can be identified and described. By then, however, it may be too late.

Another factor adding to the difficulty of identifying biological species, in addition to their sheer numbers, is the fact that they are not fixed components of the biosphere, but rather a continuously evolving complex, difficult to keep "updated" at any given moment. Species are only a small step in the evolutionary ladder, and an adequate understanding would require not only a description of the organism, but also of its previous evolutionary path and the trends for its future. The knowledge and resources are not available to allow this to be done with sufficient detail.

In dealing with cultural diversity, the problems are similar. It is possible to inventory languages. If they are not written, scripts can be invented, dictionaries can be assembled, and pronunciations and accents can be recorded. Once the language speakers are gone, however, they take with them not only the deep semantic code, which no recording can preserve, but also the basic elements that make a language — its dynamism, its changes, its role as a potential tool for social learning and innovation. Because languages are also windows to a whole imaginary universe, language extinction represents an irreversible ideological loss.

Many other elements of knowledge are being lost in the rush toward standardization and homogenization: local knowledge about plants, animals, appropriate technology, environmental and social strategies, the organization of societies and their survival in the diverse planetary environments, and spiritual approaches to nature.

Resources for the future

Although we have only incomplete knowledge about current diversities, both biological and cultural, we do know that some will become resources in the future. Perhaps the flower of a certain plant contains a substance that can be used to produce a drug to treat a serious disease that does not even exist yet. Maybe the shamans of a micronation in the Amazon know about a plant that produces a glue that is 100 times stronger than anything now known. Maybe this traditional group has a logical approach to environmental management of its particular eco-system that can be applied elsewhere. The possibilities are infinite.

All species have the potential to become resources; all present resources were part of diverse assortments in the past. We cannot know which elements are going to become resources. Societies possess a range of potential resources today, but are experiencing a number of pressures — some of them of a productive nature — that are having the effect of destroying these resources.

How can we protect our future resources? There is only one way: by protecting today's diversities. Highly diverse environments are full of potential resources that must be protected. Although low-diversity environments probably have fewer potential resources, they must also be protected because we do not know their nature and potential. In other words, all diversities must be protected. The overriding aim should be to ensure not only the well-being of today's societies, but also that the wealth of the future is not depleted.

Diversity of living systems

Diversity is the main resource of life. The future of living systems is a result of multiple current options. Diversity provides flexibility. It ensures that, even if some roads are blocked here and there, there will be alternative ways for life to continue. Uniformity is anti-life. Uniformity imparts vulnerability by not allowing other options. It can only be sustained with great investment and effort and, in the end, leads to extinction. Diversity is life; uniformity is death.

Living systems base their survival on continuous, selective adjust-ments resulting from small biological variations, genetic mutation, changes in relations in their ecosystems, and the behaviour of species, societies, and individuals. Living systems evolve in a subtly coordinated, dynamic equilibrium among thousands of diverse organisms with diverse functions that ensure the sustainability of the systems.

The elimination or modification of any component of a living system, inorganic or organic, produces changes that require a general readjustment of the system. In practice, it is difficult to know what changes will take place when one species disappears or a physical component varies; however, we do know for certain that changes will occur. Change is intrinsic to all processes and systems.

Because of the complexity of natural ecosystems, it is practically impossible to inventory all their components and still more difficult to define precisely their relations. However, although we do not know exactly how any system works, we can safely state that the strength and stability of any living system depends on the depth of its diversities and on its degree of diversity. Depth of diversity is the history that generated and allowed the development of the system's diversities, and degree of diversity is the level of differentiation or dissimilarity developed by a given system compared with others, both locally and globally. The natural tendency of local systems is to maintain their degree of diversity and to increase their depth or historical richness.

Causes and effects of the loss of natural diversity

Before industrial times, social insertion into natural complexes resulted in the use of natural diversities with only secondary negative effects. In most cases, social action adapted to the natural environments and when it did not, the societies at fault suffered the effects of their damaging actions. After the industrial revolution, societies began to use natural resources and the environment without regard for the need to sustain its productive and natural support base. The damage caused by these forces has affected not only the natural environment, but also social and cultural environments.

The impoverishment of natural systems has a more serious and widespread effect than is obvious at first. In the last decades and even now, rich, stable ecosystems with many thousands of species are being replaced with monospecific plantations that require a large investment of energy and resources to be sustained.

Plantations are essentially unstable. They are systematically invaded by "pioneers" (the agronomists call them "weeds") from neighbouring ecosystems, both plants and animals. These organisms — arriving on their own without the natural control of their predators — grow, feed, and reproduce in the new niche provided by the crop, affecting its productivity and health. In practice, there is interference between the crop and the surrounding ecosystems affecting both the ecosystems and the plantation itself. The latter functions as a new, artificial, highly unstable ecosystem.

In addition to the local organisms that adapt to the new system, plantations bring their own flora and fauna, including various plants and animals transported with the seeds or with expansion of the plantation. Crops also constantly develop diseases promoted by the concentration of individuals or seeds of a single species in reduced spaces. Viruses, bacteria, protozoa, fungi, and various parasites reproduce and thrive in the monospecific crop. Such crops require repeated treatments to prevent or cure their frequent diseases.

Pesticides are a set of toxic substances required by monospecific agriculture to eradicate undesirable biological interference. They represent one of the main tools of biological uniformity. The ideal pesticide kills everything but the crop species and, perhaps, allies, such as pollinators. As a result of their toxicity, the effects of pesticides reach far beyond the crop zone to other terrestrial and aquatic environments. For this reason, when plantations are established, a huge reduction in the diversity of all natural local systems takes place.

The forest of Misiones in South America, with tens of thousands of species, has been replaced by ecosystems based on two or three species of trees and some other species that have adapted to the change. The grasslands of Uruguay contain over 2 thousand species in each local area; the eucalyptus and pine plantations that have been introduced in prairie grasslands only contain the planted species and a few "intruders" that succeed in nesting or adapting to the new niche.

Generally speaking, when multispecific ecosystems are transformed into monospecific artificial systems, the species that manage to adapt to the new environment do so in an unbalanced manner. In some cases, without natural predators or constraints, uncontrolled growth may take place. The result is a decrease in effective and potential resources.

Diversity and culture

The concept of biodiversity includes both the range of living beings and their relations among themselves and with the physical environment. This biodiversity is dynamic, changing continuously in cycles and by evolution. Human societies are not isolated from the natural environment. They are closely interconnected with it and derive their means of existence from it. Every social group uses elements of its surrounding environment in some way. In many cases, this utilization has given rise to complex management systems that have frequently developed through long processes of trial and error. These management systems, which are based on indigenous knowledge, are often well adapted to the dynamics of natural ecosystems.

On the other hand, ecosystems are complex; they comprise innumerable relations between physical, chemical, biological, and anthropogenic factors. Traditional and popular knowledge provide some empirical indications of how the system must be treated to ensure its future health, but are often insufficient to provide the elements that are required when unexpected phenomena or unpredictable changes occur.

To ensure the sustainability of systems, scientific knowledge must also be sought (see discussion on "biodiversity and research"). However, this scientific knowledge is often more effective when is draws upon the richness of existing traditional and popular know-how. Understanding, protecting, and using biosystems in a sustainable way requires an approach that incorporates both types of knowledge. Using this approach, social groups are able to increase their pool of resources and, indirectly, their quality of life. Through this type of "empowerment through knowledge" the issue of biodiversity can be addressed to produce the most profound and positive impact on human societies.

Local cultures

Local cultures are defined by the interactions of their members with their natural environment and social history. The result is a complex web of beliefs, mythologies, and ways of looking at life, as well as multiple productive, social, and religious activities. In addition, local cultures are also a result of the successive impacts (at the local level) of successive waves of globalization, such as colonialism, at different times in history. Recently, the homogenizing influences of the communications media and transnational economic complexes are attacking the diversity of many societies. These influences operate through relatively uniform transnational cultures, taking different forms in each epoch, but widening and deepening their effects with the expansion of globalization.

Where do the elements of this transnational, standardized culture come from? Indications suggest that it is a skewed syncretism of the stronger cultures that feed on the large information and entertainment enterprises. A small number of European cultures (mainly, but not exclusively, the winners of the wars) and the large mainstream North American culture have acquired a disproportionate weight in the potpourri of world culture. Some cultures, although defeated in war, have gained a place in the mainstream through commercial or financial successes. Others have joined the international ideological complex as a result of their proximity to the cinematographic or television production sites (Mexico, for example, is close to California's film and television industry). Other peripheral and dependent cultures, removed from the international mainstream, are systematically ignored, although here and there some ideas, creations, or costumes may shyly make inroads at the edges of the transcultural global kingdom.

Uniformity against culture

On one hand, there is a steady stream of messages through the media about people with different beliefs, mores, ideologies, and behaviours that are depicted as "desirable" models; on the other, there are more and more contacts with people behaving in much the same way. As a result, small local cultures are strongly influenced by one or two

Motion pictures have become one of the main vehicles of mainstream culture during the second half of the 20th century (facade of movie theatre in downtown Tunis).

external cultures in a skewed manner, leading to a frequently irre-versible degradation of many valuable cultural elements. Like many other globalization processes, the result is a growing deformation of local cultures, with their members convinced that it is better to imitate the central cultures, reinforcing the trend toward homogeneity. If we believe that the main resources of any society are its natural and cultural diversities, we must conclude that uncontrolled and indis-criminate cultural encroachment may be a central element of social impoverishment.

Other factors worsen the situation. The central culture is not pre-sented accurately. The elements of it that are communicated are selected in an unbalanced manner, stereotyping the central societies and frequently conveying an exaggerated idea of some positive aspects (such as widespread prosperity) or sometimes promoting undesirable, negative aspects (such as exaggerated violence).

As a result, the globalizing influence tends to undermine local cultural diversity, through the imposition of stereotypes that increase the prestige of the foreign culture and devalue the local culture.

Defending local cultures

The defence of local cultures is only possible if a social framework that includes awareness of their long-term value is ensured. The richest local cultures are normally those that were locally born and nourished, that do not exist elsewhere, and are felt to be part of the authentic local heritage. It is at the traditional level that, in many places of the world, most of the richest cultures survive, frequently as valuable remnants. There is potential to consolidate within them the strength of local heritages.

Native cultures are often the result of the local and popular *brassage* of many elements, some internal, some external, producing unique, richly diverse results. The richer "elites" promote uniformity based on their economic power and their access to technology and intellectual monopolies, which have a tendency to act as factors of alienation and standardization. Poorer social sectors, on the other hand, are limited in their cultural expression to local resources, which vary from place to place and are less restricted by fashion. As a result, they often develop their own, more spontaneous and authentic cultural elements and forms of expression.

In summary, the greatest sources of diversity lie in the daily practices of their cultures by the poor and traditional communities. In most cases, these are undervalued by the "powers that be" in favour of external cultures and, for this reason, the authorities may not be the best administrators of these social resources. Consequently, a good strategy for cultural management of resources should include the training of people without this bias, who are predisposed to value popular and authentic creations, without constantly comparing them with the standards of the mainstream global culture.

To slow or stop the continuing loss of cultural diversity, it will be necessary to search, investigate, resuscitate, and revalue the elements of local heritage that have been lost in the past. Once they have been

The experience acquired and stored by this Swazi wise man, and others like him in traditional societies around the world, is an important part of absolute human knowledge.

identified, a strategy for their rescue and recuperation will have to be implemented. Finally, for any such strategy to be formulated, a creative attitude must be adopted, with less concern for the exotic or folkloric nature of diversity, and more effort on developing it, daring to imagine new forms and combinations that will enrich the social wealth.

Restoring what is lost

If we agree to merely conserve diversities, we would ensure their loss. Macroeconomic forces advance effectively and with great momentum. Slowing or stopping the processes of degradation may take too long;

most global diversities might be gone, along with the flexibility necessary for human survival. Therefore, we must develop more ambitious strategies, allowing not only conservation but also reconstruction of lost diversities.

In some cases, only small surviving testimonies or isolated species remain; in others, most elements are still present. There are cases of lost ecosystems, where most of the component species are still alive. In the case of cultures, there may be documents, oral traditions, or rituals integrated into the new standardizing cultures. Because ecosystems and cultures do not exist separately, the task must be undertaken in a holistic manner. To reconstruct a local diversity, it is necessary to restore not only the species and their relations, but also the associated culture.

Consequently, the most difficult task, but surely the most rewarding one, will be to rebuild ecocultural systems in which all the restored elements can be managed with revived cultural patterns in a recovered ideological framework, including some cultural elements of the present that, finally, will also play a role in making the survival of the recuperated systems possible.

Using the past to build the future

Rebuilding ecocultural systems presents many difficulties and challenges. First, the remnants of lost diversities may be so scarce that accurate reconstruction is impossible. Second, many reconstructed elements may interfere with elements in current complexes. Finally, reestablishing old diversities may endanger others, both old and new, that may be particularly valued by local or traditional societies.

Gaps in information about lost systems will require some imagination to design the "missing links." The new systems will certainly have new elements, including some that never existed before. However, this can be minimized by focusing on a coherent philosophical framework compatible with the system that is being restored.

Old and new visions, beliefs, myths, rituals, and feelings of populations may provide the needed elements to ensure integration and conceptual coherence of the systems. In many cases, it may be necessary to delve into every aspect of a culture to ensure that all the pieces of the puzzle are integrated harmoniously in a new complex to ensure the viability of the project.

Restoration of past diversities is a complex ecocultural process that forces choices between species, cultural patterns, and sometimes between aspects of ecology and culture. Not all options will be possible. Life is full of options, however; in each personal or collective decision, we are forced to select among several alternatives. The concept of liberty is about the opportunity to make choices among the largest number of options without interfering with others' rights to have their own range of options. In this sense, the restoration of old diversities can become a new dimension of freedom.

We have some idea of how to go about restoring diversity, but in practice, we do not know how effectively this exercise can be carried out. Common sense indicates that finding appropriate methods will not be easy. There are huge material, social, natural, historical, and ethical limitations and many reasons for not proceeding. However, the task is possible and desirable and, in the near future perhaps, we may find that it is unavoidable for survival.

The challenge is huge. So many valuable diversities have been lost. How are we to select between them? How are we to decide how much energy and resources can be dedicated to restoring an ecosystem, culture, or ecocultural complex? In many cases, the decision will be made on the basis of ethics; it will be necessary to define some values that society has ignored for a long time. We may need to restore a larger dimension of solidarity that has been forgotten in human rights declarations: solidarity with our ancestors who lost their lives and identities through ecocultural aggression and genocide and with the billions who are not yet born, but have the right to inherit not only the richest diversities of the present but also all ancient diversities.

Biodiversity and research

Despite its relevant and intrinsic values, indigenous knowledge may have important limitations, particularly in dealing with issues that span cultures or ecosystems or situations that are rapidly and unexpectedly changing. In many cases, it may be fragmented and its effectiveness significantly reduced. For these reasons, it is necessary to rescue and document the many elements of this knowledge for easy retrieval and appropriate utilization.

It is also necessary to ensure that efforts put into developing this indigenous knowledge are not simply aimed at saving it for the future. Returns from its application must go to the communities or social groups who developed the knowledge.

First, knowledge of the components and potential of existing systems must be developed using a multidisciplinary approach. Second, the identification and use of relevant traditional and popular knowledge relating to biodiversity issues must also be encouraged and supported. The focus must be on rescuing, organizing, and applying the elements of indigenous knowledge that could serve as a basis for socially and environmentally sustainable approaches to development.

Some of the issues requiring special attention include research on ecosystems, their dynamics, and components through the development of multidisciplinary teams that integrate the various mainstream scientific disciplines with the relevant elements of traditional or popular knowledge. Emphasis should be placed on holistic analysis of natural and anthropogenic systems and their specific components using an interdisciplinary and a cross-cultural approach. Development of new methods to "map" existing resources appropriately and participative design of new, imaginative models for sustainable development represent key issues that must be addressed (Table 9).

- **Aquatic biodiversity** — Special attention should be paid to the field of aquatic biodiversity because aquatic systems are currently under attack by environmentally unfriendly hydroelectric projects and other interventions. These issues should be addressed through a combined approach based on the points of view and knowledge of local groups and communities, scientific and academic elements, and resources at the national and international levels within the framework of an equitable and sustainable approach to development.

- **Valuing natural products from indigenous and local ecosystems** — Methods must be developed to assist in the identification,

Table 9. *Suggested research topics in the field of biodiversity.*

1. Ecosystems, their dynamics and components
   - Development of interdisciplinary and transcultural teams
   - Methods for ecosystem evaluation
   - Methods for inventory, analysis, modeling, resource evaluation, and conservation aspects of indigenous ecosystems
   - Methods and strategies for ecosystem management
   - Rescue, organization, and improvement of traditional, innovative, and indigenous management methods and strategies
   - Development or adaptation of other ecosystem-management methods and strategies (and integration with indigenous methods and strategies where relevant)
   - Development of methods and strategies for the protection of unique ecosystems, species, varieties, etc.

2. Management of aquatic ecosystems
   - Management of fluvial ecosystems
   - Impact of hydroelectric works on aquatic systems
   - Management of estuarine and coastal ecosystems

3. Technologies aimed at valuing natural products
   - Methods for identifying, preparing inventories for, protecting, and managing potential or actual sources of natural products
   - Technological development
   - Methods for marketing natural products

4. Preserving the cultural and genetic basis for agricultural biodiversity
   - Preservation of the germplasm of cultivated crops
   - Development of methods and strategies for rescuing and organizing indigenous agricultural knowledge

5. Protecting intellectual and property rights for indigenous knowledge
   - Protection of indigenous property and intellectual rights of new resources, products, technologies, and ideas
   - Restoration of indigenous property and intellectual rights where they have not been recognized

assessment, and use of natural resources from indigenous and local ecosystems. Emphasis must be put on resources that can be used in the framework of a sustainable approach to development and improvement of the quality of life of populations. Special attention must be paid to natural products, plant, animal, or mineral, that can be identified as resources and developed either for local use or for marketing outside the production area.

- **Preserving the cultural and genetic basis for agricultural biodiversity** — In many areas, biodiversity relates to cultural transformation of many species or varieties of plants and animals. In these situations, conservation of the basic framework of local cultures is essential to preserve the existing genetic pool. To assist in the defence of these biocultural resources, it is necessary to find ways to ensure the preservation of the germplasm of cultivated crops and develop methods and strategies for rescuing and organizing relevant indigenous agricultural knowledge.

- **Methods and strategies to ensure that indigenous and local groups obtain or benefit from the property and intellectual rights for locally developed resources, products, technologies, and ideas** — New approaches must be developed to ensure property and intellectual rights for resources, products, technologies and ideas developed as a result of the use of indigenous knowledge, particularly when these elements are used outside the local realm at national, regional, or international levels.

14

Strategies for the future

Industrial society was based on a migratory rural model. During the "industrial centuries," the relative weight of rural populations decreased systematically throughout the world. In the 20th century, the number of people living in rural areas dropped below 20% in all industrial countries.

The reasons for this are many. Rural producers began to use machines, so fewer hands were needed. Jobs were more plentiful in towns, wages were better, and careers were possible in cities. In comparison, farm work required sacrifices: milking cows on a daily basis, long hours taking care of crops and other farm chores, insufficient financial compensation. In addition, in rural areas social services, such as health care and education, were more difficult to obtain, and leisure and entertainment options were fewer and less attractive.

In developing countries, where the drive toward industrialization was delayed, the situation in rural areas was, and still is, worse: widespread unemployment, land concentrated in the hands of a few owners, inadequate housing without water or power, and poor health-care services. As a result of poor conditions in rural areas and the chance of employment in cities, massive migration to the urban centres took place. City suburbs mushroomed. Slums developed on public lands or in unsafe areas, such as floodplains or unstable slopes.

At the end of the 20th century, no country in the world is untouched by the rural–urban migration pattern. As Toffler (1981) would put it, the "second wave" is reaching the far corners of the Earth.

Decentralize decision-making

In the developed world, despite all the official discourses condemning "big government," the industrial system has, indeed, promoted extensive bureaucracies and centralized decision-making processes, both at the public and private levels. In industrial societies, central, bureaucratic and technocratic administrations control the power. Decisions about where and how to build hospitals, large high schools and colleges, hydroelectric dams and nuclear power plants, water-distribution networks, eight-lane highways, and large football stadiums are all made by the ruling, elite groups.

Together with the industrial elites, they decide upon installation of new mammoth factories, large shopping centres, supermarkets, and giant office buildings. From the beginning, policies and decisions do not give much consideration to the need to protect the environment. Industrial processes were not conceived to minimize environmental degradation. The industrial revolution has meant a general dehumanization of technology and culture, coupled with the notion that the role of humans is to control nature as if societies were independent from their home environment. In this unwise "war with nature," winning may find humankind on the losing side (Shumacher 1973).

The Third World arrived late on the industrial scene, but it arrived enthusiastically. In some of the largest developing countries, the detrimental effects of industrialization on the environment are surpassing anything that had been seen in the older industrial societies. Life is not very pleasant for workers in most Third World industrial urban societies.

The problems of industrialization in these countries are more acute because of the ideology that comes with them. Large factories, large buildings, and large hospitals are equated with progress. Growth means development, and the environment takes second place.

People value their environment

With time, in the older industrialized countries, environmental problems became so acute that civil reaction ensued. Unfortunately, it did not happen until considerable damage was done. Pristine ecosystems had been destroyed, aquifers had been contaminated beyond repair, and a whole industrial and urban effluent system had been built with little concern for the environment. However, public awareness and pressure grew to a point where decision-makers had to act. Large sums of money were spent in trying to solve the problems. In the United States, tens of billions of dollars were used in environmental correction. Environmental protection became the rule rather than the exception, and degradation seems to be under control in many areas.

In developed countries, the industrial ideology is dying. It is becoming more and more difficult to compel people to follow the banners of indiscriminate growth, modernity, and progress. Local communities and neighbourhoods have become suspicious of new projects, and they are examined through a magnifying glass. Increasingly, people are evaluating economic strategies in terms of their quality of life, and politicians are paying attention.

The idea of sustainable growth and environmental protection has not yet reached most developing regions. In many Third World countries, environmental degradation continues unabated: forests are logged and burned to make room for commercial crops or raising cattle, indigenous groups are dispossessed in the name of national sovereignty, good traditional knowledge is disappearing, and all of this is causing problems at the global level.

There is mounting evidence that environmental policies, decisions, and actions driven by increasingly globalized financial interests, with limited attention to social implications, are responsible in large measure for the destruction of the world's ability to sustain positive development processes. In the last decade of the 20th century, there are still losses at the ecosystem and cultural levels. Although the scope of damage to ecosystems is clearly critical, more significant in the long run is the loss of traditional and popular knowledge and practices in the effective. management of social, environmental, agricultural, and economic systems in communities throughout the world.

Increasingly, decisions that have an impact on local, regional, and global environments are being made by relatively fewer political and professional experts at senior national and international levels. Ironically, although such decisions are increasingly based on more sophisticated technological knowledge, they reflect an increasingly narrower range of options and less divergent perspectives.

Past approaches to development envisaged a passive receiver of grants and gifts or, at best, recipients of ready-made recipes prepared by the technocratic elites. After many failures, we now know that environmental management requires the participation of all parties concerned and incorporation of the best existing know-how, including the long-undervalued knowledge of indigenous cultures. The technological "information revolution" will only have a positive effect on the future of humankind if it succeeds in releasing all the knowledge, experience, and potential that is resident in the myriad local communities and cultures.

Problems and responsibilities are global

Current problems are not simply the result of inadequate policies in developing countries. Industrialized nations have solved or are beginning to address a number of problems at local and national levels. However, indirectly or directly, these countries are still the main contributors to the problems. They are at the centre of the standardizing culture that gradually and surely is reducing the cultural wealth that has been built up for generations at the local level. They also produce most of the carbon dioxide endangering (perhaps irreversibly) human survival; they emit most of the sulphur oxides acidifying the rain; they produce most of the chlorofluorocarbons affecting the ozone layer; and they often control the major environmentally destructive processes in developing countries. They own the factories and the technology; they consume the industrial and farming products, the wood and paper pulp, the leather, and the minerals. Last, but not least, they control the banks.

In examining the trends and defining the strategies for the future, however, it is probably immaterial to spend time searching for who is responsible for what. It will take positive thinking, large doses of imagination, and a comprehensive global effort to find our way out of the mess in which we are currently submerged. Fortunately, "we are not blind...we don't have to be driven hither and thither by the blind workings of the market, or of history, or of progress" (Shumacher 1973).

Humankind has the option of determining its own path beyond abstract notions of unavoidable trends for which responsibility cannot be demonstrated or denied. Much is to be done. Sustainable environmental management starts with the conviction that diversities should be defended, that something can be done, and that the social and political will exists to do it. This will be the main task in the years to come.

Bibliography

Anton, D. 1993. Thirsty cities: urban environments and water supply in Latin America. International Development Research Centre, Ottawa, ON, Canada. 204 pp.

Appleby, T. 1993. San Diego: turning the bulldozers on Mexican illegals. The Globe and Mail (Toronto, Canada), 16 October 1993, p. D2.

Avelima, L. 1990. Curso d'agua. Revista DAE, 50(158), 50.

Bedding, J. 1989. Money down the drain. New Scientist, 122(1660), 34–38.

Bell, D. 1973. The coming of post-industrial society: a venture in social forecasting. Basic Books, New York, NY, USA.

Bethemont, J. 1980. Geografia de la utilización de las aguas continentales. Oikos tau, Barcelona, Spain. 436 pp.

Bettson, B. 1993. Surviving the new economy. United Church Observer (New Series), 56(9), 16–23.

Bird, C. 1993. Russia's favourite fish on the verge of extinction. New Scientist, 140, 10.

Bott, R.; Brooks, D.; Robinson, J. 1983. Life after oil. Hurtig Publishers, Edmonton, AB, Canada. 203 pp.

Brown, L.R. 1993. A new era unfolds. In Brown, L.R.; et al., ed., State of the world, 1993. Worldwatch Institute, New York, NY, USA. pp. 3–21.

Business Week. 1992. The immigrants. Business Week, 3274 (13 July 1992), p. 116.

Calva Téllez, J.L. 1992. Efectos de un tratado de libre comercio en el sector agropecuario mexicano. In Pablos, J., ed., La agricultura mexicana frente al tratado trilateral de libre comercio. Centro de Investigaciones Económicas, Sociales y Tecnológicas de la Agroindustria y de la Agricultura, Universidad Autónoma de Chapingo, Mexico City, Mexico. pp. 13–32.

Castillo Berthier, H.F. 1983. La sociedad de la basura: caciquismo en la ciudad de México. Universidad Nacional Autónoma de México, Mexico City, Mexico. Cuadernos de Investigación Social. 142 pp.

CETESB (Companhia Estadual de Tecnologia de Saneamento Básico e de Defensa do Meio Ambiente). 1992. El aire que respiramos. Secretariá del Medio Ambiente, Gobierno del Estado de São Paulo, São Paulo, Brazil. 24 pp.

Charles, D. 1993. In search of a better burn. New Scientist, 140(1857), 20–41.

Chovin, P.; Roussel, A. 1968. La pollution atmospherique. Presses Universitaires de France, Paris, France.

CIDAC (Centro de Investigación para el Desarrollo A.C.). 1991. El acuerdo libre comercio México–Estados Unidos: alternativas para el futuro: camino para fortalecer la soberanía. 2nd ed. Editorial Diana S.A. de C.V., Mexico City, Mexico. 291 pp.

Cloud, P.; Gibor, A. 1970. The oxygen cycle. Scientific American, 223(3), 57–68.

Colinvaux, P.A. 1989. The past and future Amazon. Scientific American, 260(5), 102–108.

Cortés, D.E. 1993. Superó el sector maquilador al petrolero en generación de ingresos. El Universal (Mexico City), 9 September 1993, p. 3.

Cortés, A.; Jaimes, L.R.; Farvolden, R.N. 1989. Hidrología isotópica de la influencia de una tormenta en la descarga natural del agua subterránea en la Sierra de Monte alto. Geofísica Internacional, 28(2), 435–449.

DAEE (Departamento de Aguas e Energia Eléctrica do São Paulo), Asesoria Recursos Hídricos. 1988. Agua subterrânea: reserva estratégica. Aguas e Energia Eléctrica, 5(13), 14–23.

Dewar, H. 1993. Algae crisis deepens in Florida Bay. The Miami Herald, 25 July 1993, p. B1.

Economist, The. 1993a. A survey of the frontiers of finance: the mathematics of markets. The Economist, 329(7832), 3.

———— 1993b. Across the Rio Grande. The Economist, 329(7832), 67.

———— 1993c. Malaysia: not yet out of the woods. The Economist, 329(7833), 64–65.

———— 1994a. The new colonizers. The Economist, 332(7875), 32.

———— 1994b. The tragedy of the oceans. The Economist, 330(7855), 23–28.

———— 1994c. Nigeria on the brink. The Economist, 332(7875), 33.

Elmer-Dewitt, P. 1994. Battle for the soul of the Internet. Time, 144(4), 40–46.

El País. 1992. Emigración de los desesperados: las nuevas invasiones africanas. El País (Montevideo, Uruguay), 27 November 1992, p. 2.

Erhart, H. 1968. La genèse des sols entant que phénomène géologique. Masson, Paris, France.

FAO (Food and Agriculture Organization of the United Nations). 1988. FAO yearbook, 1988. FAO, Rome, Italy.

Fearnside, P.M.; Tebaldi Tardin, A.; Meira Filho, L.G. 1990. Deforestation rate in Brazilian Amazonia. Instituto de Pesquisas Espaciais, São José dos Campos, Brazil. 8 pp.

Funk & Wagnalls. 1994. The world almanac and book of facts. Funk & Wagnalls, Inc., New York, NY, USA. 551 pp.

Gardner, J.A. 1977. Urbanization in Brazil: international urbanization survey report. Ford Foundation, New York, NY, USA.

Gibbons, J.H.; Blair, P.D.; Gwin, H.L. 1989. Strategies for energy use. Scientific American, 261(3), 136–144.

Goldenberg, J.; Johansson, T.B.; Reddy, A.K.N.; Williams, R.H. 1988. Energy for a sustainable world. Wiley Eastern Ltd, New Delhi, India. 517 pp.

Gómez Cruz, M.A.; Schwentesius Rindermann, R.; Merino Sepúlveda, A. 1992. La producción de hortalizas en México frente al tratado de libre comercio con EE.UU. y Canadá. In Pablos, J., ed., La agricultura mexicana frente al tratado trilateral de libre comercio. Centro de Investigaciones Económicas, Sociales y Tecnológicas de la Agroindustria y de la Agricultura, Universidad Autónoma de Chapingo, Mexico City, Mexico. pp. 33–62.

Gonzalez Moran, I.; Rodriguez Castillo, R. 1989. Monitoreo geofísico en el entorno de un basurero industrial de desechos de cromo. Geofísica International, 28(2), 409–416.

Graedel, T.E.; Crutzen, P.J. 1989. Managing planet Earth. Scientific American, 261(3), 58–69.

Granados Velazco, A. 1988. Invasión que pone en peligro los mantos acuíferos del Sur. Diario El Dia (Mexico City), 20 March 1988, metropolitan supplement 10(3796).

Gray, J. 1993. Need for power supply spells doom for Armenian lake. The Globe and Mail (Toronto, Canada), 11 September 1993, p. A9.

Gutierrez, M.O.; Caffera, R.; Cespedes, C.; Gonzalez, A.; Panario, D. 1993. Hacia una evaluación de efectos ambientales de la forestación en Uruguay con especies introducidas. In Perez Arrarte, C., ed., Desarrollo forestal y medio ambiente. Editorial Hemisferio Sur, Montevideo, Uruguay. pp. 157–206.

Hahn, S.K.; Ker, A.D.R. 1980. Foreword. In Root crops in Eastern Africa: proceedings of a workshop held in Kigali, Rwanda, 23–27 November 1980. International Development Research Centre, Ottawa, ON, Canada. IDRC-177e, pp. 5–6.

Hermann, R.M. 1979. Alternative proposals for water quality management in greater São Paulo, Brazil. In Biswas, A.K., ed., Water management and environment in Latin America. Pergamon Press, Oxford, UK. pp. 273–284.

Herrera, I. 1989. El sistema acuífero de la Cuenca de México. Geofísica Internacional, 28(2), 2.

Herrera, I.; Yates, R.; Hennart, J.P. 1982. Estudio de hundimiento y balance de los acuíferos subterráneos a la Ciudad de México. Instituto de

Investigaciones en Matemáticas Aplicadas y Sistemas, Universidad Nacional Autónoma de México, Mexico City, Mexico.

Kerkhof, P. 1992. Reforestation around wells in northern Senegal. *In* Foley, G.; Barnard, G., ed., Agroforestry in Africa: a survey of project experience. Panos Ltd, London, UK. 216 pp.

Lents, J.M.; Kelly, W.J. 1993. Clearing the air in Los Angeles. Scientific American, 269(4), 32–39.

Lonergan, S.C.; Brooks, D.B. 1994. Watershed: the role of fresh water in the Israeli–Palestinian conflict. International Development Research Centre, Ottawa, ON, Canada. 314 pp.

Lovelock, J. 1988. The ages of Gaia: a biography of our living earth. W.W. Norton and Co., New York, NY, USA. 252 pp.

Mariani Neto, F.; Ganzili, J.P.; Sakurai, K.; de Souza, O. 1988. Tendencias de industrialização no interior do Estado de São Paulo. Revista Companhia Estadual de Tecnologia de Saneamento Básico e de Defesa do Meio Ambiente, 2(2).

Maurits la Rivière, J.M. 1989. Threats to the world's water: the Rhine. Scientific American, 261(3), 80–94.

Meadows, D.H.; Meadows, D.L.; Randers, J. 1992. Beyond the limits. Earthscan Ltd, London, UK. 300 pp.

Mougeot, L.J.A. 1988. Hydroelectric development and involuntary resettlement in Brazilian Amazonia: planning and evaluation. Cobham Resource Consultants, Edinburgh, UK. 106 pp.

National Geographic. 1986. The making of America: northern plains (map 13 of 17). Cartographic Division, National Geographic Society, Washington, DC, USA.

Ortega, A. 1988. Analysis of regional groundwater flow and boundary conditions in the basin of Mexico. University of Waterloo, Waterloo, ON, Canada. Master's thesis. 45 pp.

Pearce, D.; Barbier, E.; Markandya, A. 1990. Sustainable development. Chapter 6: Natural resources in the economy of the Sudan. Edward Elgar Publishing House, Aldershot, Hants, UK.

Pearce, F. 1991. Africa at a watershed. New Scientist, 129(1761), 34–40.

——— 1994a. Neighbours sign deal to save Aral Sea. New Scientist, 141(1909), 10.

——— 1994b. How disappearing lakes are swelling the oceans. New Scientist, 141(1909), 17.

Perez Arrarte, C. 1993. Desarrollo forestal? Una aproximación convencional. *In* Perez Arrarte, C., ed., Desarrollo forestal y medio ambiente. Editorial Hemisferio Sur, Montevideo, Uruguay. pp. 9–54.

Poore, M.E.D.; Fries, C. 1987. Efectos ecológicos de los eucaliptos. Food and Agriculture Organization of the United Nations, Rome, Italy. FAO Technical Study No. 59.

Preston, J. 1991. Deforestation in the Amazon. The Washington Post (Washington, DC), 17 March 1991, p. A35.

Reisner, M. 1986. The Cadillac desert. Penguin Books, New York, NY, USA. 582 pp.

Ryan, M.C. 1989. An investigation of inorganic nitrogen compounds in the groundwater in the valley of Mexico. Geofísica Internacional, 28(2), 417–434.

Salati, E. 1991. A região amazonica e as mudanças globais: necessidade de um plano de pesquisas. Paper presented at the IDRC Meeting on Environmental Policies, Manaus, Montevideo, Uruguay, January 1991. International Development Research Centre, Regional Office for Latin America and the Caribbean, Montevideo, Uruguay.

Salati, E.; Nobre, C.A. 1991. Possible climatic impacts of tropical deforestation. Climatic Change, 19, 177–196.

Secretaría de Desarrollo Social. 1993. Informe de la situación general en materia de equilibrio ecológico y protección al medio ambiente. Instituto Nacional de Ecología, Mexico City, Mexico.

Serril, M.S. 1994 The poisoned Amazon. Time, 143(2), 28–29.

Sharda V.N.; et al. 1988. Hydrological behavior of the Nilgiri sub-watersheds as affected by bluegums plantations: Part II. Monthly water balances at different rainfall and run-off probabilities. Forestry Abstracts, 50(5), 298 (Abstract 2779).

Shumacher, E.F. 1973. Small is beautiful: economics as if people mattered. Harper and Row, New York, NY, USA. 324 pp.

Shuttleworth, W.J. 1988. Evaporation from Amazonian rain forest. Proceedings of the Royal Society (B), 233, 321–346.

Souza dos Santos, O., ed. 1988. A cultura da soja-1 (coleção do agricultor). Publicaçoes Globo Rural, Rio de Janeiro, Brazil. 133 pp.

Stern, A. 1993. Where the lunar winds blow free. Astronomy, 21(11), 36–41.

Time. 1993. Nigeria: shattered dream. Time, 142(10), 36.

Toffler, A. 1981. The third wave. Bantam, New York, USA. 537 pp.

————— 1990. Powershift. Bantam, New York, NY, USA. 611 pp.

UNDP (United Nations Development Programme). 1994. World development report 1994. UNDP, New York, NY, USA.

Varea, A. 1992. Petroecuador: conciencia petrolera. El Comercio (Quito, Ecuador), 23 August 1992, p. B10.

World Bank; UNDP (United Nations Development Programme); Commission of the European Communities; FAO (Food and Agriculture Organization of the United Nations). 1993. Fish for the future: a study of international fisheries research (summary report). World Bank, Washington, DC, USA.

WRI (World Resources Institute). 1992. World resources 1992–1993. Oxford University Press, New York, USA.

About the Author

Danilo J. Anton, a Uruguayan–Canadian geographer, received his doctorate in 1973 from the Université Louis Pasteur in Strasbourg, France. His distinguished career has taken him from Saudi Arabia, to Mexico, to Uruguay, to Canada. In Dhahran, Saudi Arabia, Dr Anton managed the Sand Research Program and was Coordinator of the Geology and Mineral Division of the University of Petroleum and Minerals. In Mexico, he taught marine geology and geomorphology in Acapulco and managed the Center for Geographical Research in Guerrero. In Uruguay, he was Director of the Geography Department at the Faculty of Sciences of the University of Montevideo. And, in Canada, he spent several years as a consultant specializing in water issues, eventually joining IDRC. On behalf of IDRC, Dr Anton has initiated and monitored many successful projects in Africa, Asia, and Latin America, particularly in the fields of alternative water resources and environmental management. Dr Anton is widely published in the fields of geomorphology, hydrogeology, and environmental science. His most recent published work includes revisionist texts on South American history and the IDRC book *Thirsty Cities: Urban Environments and Water Supply in Latin America* (1993), which deals with the environmental problems of Southern megalopolises and whose video version has been presented on public television in Canada and many other countries around the world.

About the Institution

The International Development Research Centre (IDRC) is a public corporation created by the Parliament of Canada in 1970 to support technical and policy research to help meet the needs of developing countries. The Centre is active in the fields of environment and natural resources, social sciences, health sciences, and information sciences and systems. Regional offices are located in Africa, Asia, Latin America, and the Middle East.

About the Publisher

IDRC BOOKS publishes research results and scholarly studies on global and regional issues related to sustainable and equitable development. As a specialist in development literature, IDRC BOOKS contributes to the body of knowledge on these issues to further the cause of global understanding and equity. IDRC publications are sold through its head office in Ottawa, Canada, as well as by IDRC's agents and distributors around the world.